Praise for *The Hidden Power of Silence in the Mass*

"In this time of Eucharistic revival, Fr. Boniface Hicks, O.S.B., has made a significant contribution to the effort in his book *The Hidden Power of Silence in the Mass*. I have long believed that priests, deacons, lay ecclesial ministers, and the faithful need to enter more deeply and reverently into the mystery we celebrate in the Eucharistic sacrifice. Fr. Hicks's profound reflections on the various moments in the celebration of the Mass will certainly help us do that, awakening the "Eucharistic amazement" called for by Pope St. John Paul II."

—**The Most Reverend Alexander K. Sample**
Archbishop of the Archdiocese of Portland in Oregon

"Silence is a gift of God, to let us speak more intimately with Him" (St. Vincent Pallotti). At the hands of Mary and St. Benedict the spiritual master Fr. Boniface Hicks, O.S.B., expertly guides us to a deeper appreciation of silence as elemental for "full and active participation" (SC 14) in the Mass. The mind of Mary is *the* indispensable paradigm to discover anew silence as richly filled with content. Using Prosper Guéranger, Romano Guardini, St. John Paul II, Benedict XVI, and Pope Francis, the author most ably translates the art of liturgical silence into the contemporary idiom. This precious book is a timely reminder that there is something joyfully sacrificing and—more importantly—welcoming about Eucharistic silence. I highly recommend this book for the beautiful project of personal Eucharistic renewal.

—**Fr. Emery de Gaál, Ph.D.**
University of St. Mary of the Lake/Mundelein Seminary

"If silence is a symbol of the world to come (as the *Catechism* teaches), and the Mass truly participates in this next world, then we ought to experience silence—and Heaven—at Mass. Fr. Boniface Hicks does the praying Church a great service in promoting and teaching silence. Both priests and laypeople will benefit from a deeper appreciation of this rich and necessary element of the sacred liturgy. Were silence simply an absence of noise or sound, perhaps such a treatment of the topic wouldn't be necessary. But liturgical silence—true, authentic, positive—is anything but a void. Indeed, as Fr. Boniface shows, silence reveals God Himself so that we may encounter him most profoundly."

—Christopher Carstens
**Office for Sacred Worship, Diocese of La Crosse, Wisconsin;
editor and publisher of *Adoremus Bulletin***

"This book is a cry from the Holy Spirit. This cry has been heard by Fr. Boniface; now it must be heard by all priests. The silence in the Mass is not a pause in a ritual to catch our breath. Silence, indeed, carries to our souls the very breath of the Spirit. Here in the silences of the Mass, a community of faith is loved by the divine, healed by this love, and called to a mission of love within today's culture. This is a substantive work that seminarians can internalize and so lead a new generation of priests who promote generous silence as intrinsic to true worship."

—Deacon James Keating, Ph.D.
**Professor of spiritual theology,
Kenrick-Glennon Seminary, St. Louis, Missouri**

"Criticism of the celebration of the contemporary Roman Eucharistic liturgy is that it becomes an almost unbroken flow or a barrage of spoken and sung words. In this excellent book in which he truly shares his heart, Fr. Boniface Hicks, O.S.B., evokes the silence that is the ground of possibility of the spoken word and all physical noise, and especially the divine silence, which is the possibility of any interior word and interior listening. Fr. Boniface shows not only where silence is provided and intended in the Roman Rite but how to pray in that silence.

—Fr. Thomas Acklin, O.S.B.,
author of *The Unchanging Heart of the Priesthood*

"This book is a beautiful corrective. Catholics have too long emphasized the adornments of the Mass while backgrounding its essence. Yet the Seer says of heavenly worship: "When the Lamb opened the seventh seal, there was silence in heaven for about half an hour" (Rev. 8:1). Such silence begins in the heart. When we have learned it, we will recover our sense of Presence.

—Mike Aquilina, author of *The Mass of the Early Christians*

"It is evident that the Holy Spirit not only inspired but also accompanied Fr. Boniface as he prayerfully penned *The Hidden Power of Silence in the Mass*. There is no greater act of love at this time in Church history than assisting each other in praying the Mass, particularly the silence of the Mass. For it is in these silent depths that we discover the communion we so desperately long for, satisfied by the loving embrace of the Trinity and uniting us to one another as we experience a taste of Heaven on earth. Can you imagine how radiantly the Church would shine if each one of us—her members—allowed our hearts to be drawn into the depths of liturgical silence? That is a beauty I desperately long to behold!

—Sr. Alicia Torres, F.E., National Eucharistic Revival Executive Team; managing editor, *Heart of the Revival* newsletter

"*The Hidden Power of Silence in the Mass* will fill your heart, mind, body, and soul with goodness, truth, and beauty. In this book, Fr. Boniface skillfully connects the realities that are present in the various aspects of silence in the Mass with the ache of every human heart. As you tarry through these pages, you will want to savor each morsel of silence, pray more deeply, adore and receive the Lord more fully, and wholly encounter the One who loves you like no other.

—Sr. Miriam James Heidland, S.O.L.T.

"In *The Hidden Power of Silence in the Mass*, Fr. Hicks has created a refuge for every follower of Jesus to return to the simplicity and purity of silence. With beautiful illustrations and gentle invitations to engage in different types of silence, we rediscover more of ourselves and experience more of God in wonderful ways. An insightful and transformative read!"

—Sarah Kaczmarek
Director of Pastoral Ministry, Encounter Ministries

The Hidden Power of Silence
in the Mass

Also by Fr. Boniface Hicks
from Sophia Institute Press:

*The Fruit of Her Womb: 33-Day Preparation
for Total Consecration to Jesus*

Fr. Boniface Hicks, O.S.B.

THE HIDDEN POWER OF *Silence* IN THE MASS

A Guide for Encountering Christ in the Liturgy

SOPHIA INSTITUTE PRESS

Manchester, New Hampshire

Sophia Institute Press
Box 5284, Manchester, NH 03108
1-800-888-9344
www.SophiaInstitute.com

Sophia Institute Press is a registered trademark of Sophia Institute.

paperback ISBN 979-8-88911-108-5

ebook ISBN 979-8-88911-109-2

Library of Congress Control Number: 2024903405

Third printing

For my monastic community,
the Benedictine monks of St. Vincent Archabbey
in Latrobe, Pennsylvania, in whose company
I have learned to love the liturgy

Contents

Foreword

The Eucharist is the heart of the Church. If the Church is strong in her Eucharistic life, then she will be strong. If her Eucharistic life is weak, she will be weak. A Eucharistic Revival seeks to strengthen the Church for whom she is called to be in the world today. Pope Leo XIII, the great pope who ushered in the twentieth century, believed that the Church was entering into one of the most difficult times of her history. He knew the Church needed to be strengthened for the struggle ahead, and he decided, near the end of his pontificate, to write an encyclical letter on the Eucharist. He believed that the most important way to strengthen the Church for the time that was coming would be through a renewal of Eucharistic fervor:

> Now nothing can be better adapted to promote a renewal of the strength and fervor of faith in the human mind than the mystery of the Eucharist, the "mystery of faith," as it has been most appropriately called. For in this one mystery the entire supernatural order, with all its wealth and variety of wonders, is in a manner summed up and contained.[1]

[1]   Pope Leo XIII, encyclical *Mirae Caritatis* (May 28, 1902), no. 7.

The Hidden Power of Silence in the Mass

The supernatural order of the world and our lives is summed up and contained in the Eucharist. From the Mass we learn to see truly ourselves, our lives, and the world in which we live. If we are going to have a true revival of the Church in our day, we must learn to enter deeply into the mystery of the Eucharist, as Pope Leo XIII encourages us to do. Learning to live the Eucharist will bring about a new Christ-centered vision that will bring true revival to our hearts and allow us to bring this fire of love to our world.

We develop a Christ-centered vision through an encounter with Jesus Christ living in the Eucharist. Jesus lives in the Eucharist and gives Himself for us and to us. It is important for every Christian to realize that Jesus Christ is not just a personality or an object of study but a living Person who longs to encounter us. The Eucharist is not just a communal prayer, or an official ritual, but it is the prayer of Jesus Christ and it is the place where we can encounter Him. And when we encounter Jesus, it changes everything, it "gives life a new horizon and a decisive direction."[2] Unfortunately, many people who attend Mass have not had such an encounter with the living Jesus. As St. Teresa of Calcutta wrote to all her spiritual daughters, the Missionaries of Charity, in her Varanasi Letter of 1993:

> I worry some of you still have not really met Jesus—one to one—you and Jesus alone. We may spend time in chapel—but have you seen with the eyes of your soul how He looks at you with love? Do you really know the living Jesus—not from books but from being with Him in your heart? Have you heard the loving words He speaks to you? Ask for the grace, He is longing simply to give it. Until you

---

[2] Pope Benedict XVI, encyclical *Deus Caritas Est* (December 25, 2005), no. 1.

can hear Jesus in the silence of your own heart, you will not be able to hear Him saying "I Thirst" in the hearts of the poor.

Mother Teresa was writing this to the consecrated women in her religious order, who were doing wonderful and inspiring works of mercy for the poor. Despite their works of mercy, Mother Teresa was not sure they really knew Jesus. Unless we learn to live from our personal encounter with the love of God in Jesus Christ, even great works of mercy will fall flat. They will be like salt that has lost its savor. For this reason, Pope Francis summons us: "I invite all Christians, everywhere, at this very moment, to a renewed personal encounter with Jesus Christ."[3] As we deepen our personal encounter with Jesus Christ in the Eucharist, we will be changed. We will become more and more like Jesus.

This is what the Mass wants to teach us. In the Mass, Christ gives Himself to the Father for us, and He wants to teach us to make a gift of our lives with Him. This is why He makes His sacrifice, His Passion, death, and Resurrection, present in the Mass. We call this the Paschal Mystery, and it becomes present at every Mass so we can live from it and learn to offer our lives with Christ. In this way, the Mass teaches us the value of our own suffering. Our suffering, too, can have real meaning. Just like Jesus' suffering, it can be part of the redemption of the world—if we learn to live the Paschal Mystery ourselves. As Pope Francis says, "It is the gift of the Paschal Mystery of the Lord which, received with docility, makes our life new."[4]

---

[3] Pope Francis, apostolic exhortation *Evangelii Gaudium* (November 24, 2013), no. 3.

[4] Pope Francis, apostolic letter *Desiderio Desideravi* (June 29, 2022), no. 20.

Uniting our suffering to Christ's with faith gives value to our suffering. This is what Pope Benedict says the Eucharist wants to do in us. "The Eucharist draws us into Jesus' act of self-oblation. More than just statically receiving the incarnate *Logos*, we enter into the very dynamic of his self-giving."[5] The Eucharist wants to turn us into lovers. It wants to teach us the value of our sufferings. Through the Mass, our sufferings can help to save the world because they become part of Jesus' perfect worship of the Father on the Cross. Nothing else can give such value to our lives.

But here is the key to fully living a Eucharistic life, and the reason the book you hold is so important. We will not be able to enter into this encounter with Jesus Christ living in the Eucharist, we will not be able to learn to unite our suffering with His, if we do not learn silent listening. Uniting our hearts to the Heart of Jesus in the Eucharist is an interior work. This interior work takes place particularly in silence:

> We need to be conscious of the gift we have received, a gift that is none other than the Lord himself in his act of self-giving. We become conscious of this gift when we actively engage our minds, hearts, and bodies to every part of the liturgy, allowing God through the words, actions, gestures, and even the moments of silence to speak to us. We actively and consciously participate by giving our full attention to the words being spoken in the prayers and the Scriptures, even if we have heard them hundreds of times before.[6]

As St. Thomas Aquinas expressed in the hymn we sing for Eucharistic Benediction, faith substitutes for the failure of our

---

[5]   *Deus Caritas Est*, no. 13.

[6]   USCCB, *The Mystery of the Eucharist in the Life of the Church*, no. 31.

senses. It is especially in silence through faith, as our senses fail to take in the full reality, that we are able to encounter Christ, to unite our sacrifices with His, to adore Him and to abide in His presence. This book will help you to enter into each of those movements of silent prayer. By learning to pray the silence of the Mass, we can learn to live a more Eucharistic life and participate in the revival that the Lord wants to bring about. This silence is not passive! No, it is active participation, actively centering our hearts on the Lord to be united with Him. The result of learning to pray in this silence will be that our hearts are set on fire as the heart of Jesus is in the Eucharist.

Revival is a work of God. Revival is a divine visitation. It is a sovereign work of God in response to prolonged and prevailing prayer. Pentecost was a revival. Mary and the apostles gathered in the upper room, the same room where Jesus celebrated the first Mass, and they asked for the Holy Spirit to come. When He came, He transformed them and through them He transformed the world.

Fr. Boniface Hicks's *The Hidden Power of Silence in the Mass* can play an important role in bringing about this revival in our hearts, as it inspires a greater faith in us and teaches us how to enter more deeply into the heart of the Mass. Let us ask God that through our actively entering into the encounter with God in silence He might bring about a great revival of Eucharistic faith in our Church, so that we might be who God calls us to be in the twenty-first century.

—The Most Reverend Andrew Cozzens
Bishop of the Diocese of Crookston
Chairman of the 2024 National Eucharistic Congress

Introduction

For while gentle silence enveloped all things,
and night in its swift course was now half gone,
thy all-powerful word leaped from heaven,
from the royal throne,
into the midst of the land that was doomed,
a stern warrior. (Wisd. 18:14–15)

Pope Benedict XVI saw the need for an education in silence in our time: "Ours is not an age which fosters recollection; at times one has the impression that people are afraid of detaching themselves, even for a moment, from the mass media. For this reason, it is necessary nowadays that the People of God be educated in the value of silence."[7] How can we bring about this education in the value of silence?

Silence is an overloaded term that can be studied from many perspectives. We can speak about sound waves, and we can measure these sound waves to rate various noise levels using the metric of decibels. In this way, we can identify the "most silent" place

---

[7]   Pope Benedict XVI, post-synodal apostolic exhortation *Verbum Domini* (September 30, 2010), no. 66.

in the world.[8] We could call this lack of sound waves "physical silence" because it is simply a matter of physics. Physical silence is impersonal, so it does not capture the dimensions of silence that we are most interested in when speaking about the spiritual life. When speaking about silence as a human phenomenon, we are interested primarily in interior silence. In contrast to the decibels of physical silence, a "personal silence" or "interpersonal silence" is always in reference to words, in the sense of communication. Twitter, for example, does not produce decibels, but it does interrupt personal silence.

Physical silence and personal silence can coexist, of course, but they are clearly distinct. For example, a man could be standing in the most silent place in the world and still lack personal silence, as he experiences a flood of words in his mind. Likewise, a deaf person who always experiences the world as being physically silent could be overwhelmed by the number of words he is receiving from a room full of people speaking in sign language. Contrariwise, a person in a jungle filled with physical sounds could experience an interior, personal silence that is free from words. Or, again, a person hearing the high decibels of a waterfall could enjoy an

---

[8] "According to *Guinness World Records*, the anechoic chamber at Orfield Laboratories in Minneapolis is the quietest place in the world, with a background noise reading of –9.4 decibels. If you chatted with someone, your speech would measure around 60 decibels on a sound-level meter. If you stood quietly on your own in a concert hall, the meter would drop down to a level of about 15 decibels. The threshold of hearing, the quietest sound a young adult can hear, is about 0 decibels. The test room at Orfield Laboratories, like the chamber at Salford University, is far quieter than that." Trevor Cox, "Quietest Places in the World," *American Scientist* 102, no. 5 (September–October 2014): 382.

interior silence in the peace of his heart as he gazes on the beauty of order in nature.

The philosopher Bernard Dauenhauer describes silence as a cut in our inner stream of experience:

> Dauenhauer notes that discourse always finds a pre-predicative stream of experience which is essentially endless and never fully determinate. He terms this feature the "and so forth" of experience.... The shift from the "and so forth" to discourse involves a "cutting" into that otherwise endless progression. The "cut" is not, in the first instance, word, but silence.[9]

There is undoubtedly a relationship between physical silence and personal silence, as noted by Cardinal Robert Sarah: "Just as interior asceticism cannot be obtained without concrete mortifications, it is absurd to speak about interior silence without exterior silence."[10] Exterior silence creates an experience that can lead to interior silence by first leading to interior awareness. As Fr. Réginald Garrigou-Lagrange described it: "From the moment he ceases to converse with his fellow men, man converses interiorly with himself about what preoccupies him most."[11] This internal stream of words in man's conversation with himself can be drawn

---

[9] Forrest Williams, "Review of *Silence: The Phenomenon and Its Ontological Significance* by Bernard P. Dauenhauer," *Philosophical Topics* 12, no. 3 (Winter 1981): 236–240.

[10] Cardinal Robert Sarah and Nicolas Diat, *The Power of Silence: Against the Dictatorship of Noise* (San Francisco: Ignatius Press, 2017), no. 19, e-book.

[11] Réginald Garrigou-Lagrange, O.P., *The Three Ages of the Interior Life: Prelude of Eternal Life*, trans. Sr. M. Timothea Doyle, O.P., vol. 1 (Saint Louis: B. Herder, 1947), e-book.

steadily into conversation with God: "As soon as a man seriously seeks truth and goodness, this intimate conversation with himself tends to become conversation with God."[12] Furthermore, because God is beyond all finite words — indeed, it could be said that the language of God is silence[13] — this interior conversation tends more and more to interior silence.

In reflecting on personal silence, we could further differentiate several kinds of silence. There is a basic difference between the types of positive silence, in which beauty can grow, and the types of negative silence that can be used as a defense (the silent treatment). Within the types of positive silence, we identify five:

- *ascetical silence*, a preparation, making room to receive
- *mystical silence*, an encounter that happens through listening
- *sacrificial silence*, the self-gift that forms the response to the encounter
- *contemplative silence*, adoration and communion
- *eternal silence*, a timeless savoring of the communion

These silences follow a basic flow that moves from making space (ascetical) to abiding in transforming union (eternal). This fivefold movement is creative, serving as the pattern in which life came forth on this earth and the pattern through which divine life comes forth in the soul. It is the pattern of Creation in Genesis, the pattern of the Incarnation in Mary, the pattern of silences in the Mass, and the pattern of transformation in our souls.

---

[12]   Ibid.

[13]   Sarah and Diat write: "The sound of the silence in God allows us to learn the first note of this canticle which is the song of the heavens. 'The language [God] best hears is silent love,' John of the Cross says magnificently in his *Maxims on Love*." *The Power of Silence*, no. 82.

This pattern of movements in silence appears in the first account of Creation. First, there is a silence that precedes the Word and, in a sense, prepares for it: "The earth was without form and void" (Gen. 1:2). We might say that this void is *listening* so as to hear the Word, and then there is the moment the silence encounters the Word: "God said, 'Let there be light.'" The silence yields to the Word (gives itself in response, so to speak) so that a new reality comes into being: "And there was light" (Gen. 1:3). This new reality is now a mystery that can be divinely pondered in the silence—"And God saw everything that he had made"—and savored: "and behold, it was very good" (Gen. 1:31). This is the pattern of Creation. In this original pattern, the silence does not have free will, so the listening and yielding happen automatically.

In the Redemption, God cooperates with Mary's free will and makes a new creation in the silence of her womb. We can trace the same movements of silence as in the original Creation. First, Mary makes space: created without sin, she presents no hindrance to the Word. Through listening, she encounters the Word first through the angel who announced His coming. Then, in response, she offers herself in silence to receive the Word. This gives birth to a mystery beyond words in contemplative silence. Finally, Mary is left in silence to savor tenderly the mystery that had been conceived in silence. These are the movements of silence: preparing for the Word, encountering the Word, offering oneself in response to the Word, birthing a mystery that transcends words, and tenderly savoring the mystery. These are the movements not only of the Blessed Virgin Mary, the woman of silence, but also of the Church, especially in her liturgy, and these movements steadily form the heart of every believer who is willing to enter into the Church's liturgy.

In these movements, we can see an alternation of action and reception. The active preparation, creation of a space, and waiting are followed by a silence of encounter, which is reception. Mary does not create the encounter, only the space, but then the encounter happens to her as she listens in silence. Her response is an action, a self-offering in silence. This is followed by another silence that happens to her, a conception, which moves her to adoration. Her final action is savoring, to remain with the Word, now conceived within her, in silence. The difference between encounter and conception lies in the response—a movement to the action of self-offering, in the case of encounter, or a kind of completion that moves to savoring the gift, in the case of conception (which, in the liturgy, is experienced as adoration and communion).

The Church's liturgy in the Roman Rite uses intentional periods of physical silence to capture and foster these various movements of personal silence. These are intended to provide a "cutting" in the interior stream of experience so as to foster a movement in the heart of the believer in relationship to the Word. The better we understand the rationale behind these ritual gestures of liturgical silence, the better we will be able to correspond with them and so be transformed by the Word in our liturgical worship.

The Church's liturgy engages silence in each of the ways just listed, and this will provide a structure for our reflections in this book. Prior to Mass and in the Introductory Rites, the participant is encouraged to foster an ascetical silence to prepare space for encountering the Word (chapter 2). Then, in a mystical silence, the participant encounters the voice of God in the Liturgy of the Word (chapter 3). This invites a response of self-offering in a sacrificial silence (chapter 4). Following the self-offering, the Word becomes incarnate in the participant and really present on the altar and is adored and received in contemplative silence (chapter 5). Finally, the participant remains in a timeless or eternal silence to savor the divine presence (chapter 6).

Before entering into the specific dimensions of praying through the movements of silence in the liturgy, we will look more generally, in chapter 1, at the dynamics of silence in personal prayer and the Church's prescriptions for silence in the liturgy. We will conclude each chapter with a look at the example of Mary as the supreme model of silence for us. We will also learn from a great saint of silence and a lover of liturgy, St. Benedict. Additionally, I will provide concrete practices to foster the movement of silence discussed in the chapter.

To conclude our introduction, let us consider a summary invitation by Pope Benedict XVI, who captures each of the dimensions we highlight—the purification, listening, offering, bringing to birth, and contemplation:

> How can we open the world, and first of all ourselves, to the Word without entering into the silence of God from which his Word proceeds? For the purification of our words, hence, also for the purification of the words of the world, we need that silence which becomes contemplation, which introduces us into God's silence and brings us to the point where the Word, the redeeming Word, is born.[14]

---

[14] Pope Benedict XVI, Homily at a Eucharistic Concelebration with the Members of the International Theological Commission, October 6, 2006.

1

Silence in Prayer

Silence is a hallmark of prayer in many religious traditions. It carries with it a certain awe, as if maintaining extended periods of silence were supernatural in itself, but in reality, it is part of the human life's natural commute from solitude to encounter. Silence creates a separation that allows one to move away from an external focus on human activity and enter more fully into an interior dialogue.

The experience of silence is that the human spirit begins naturally to rise toward God or go deeper inward, where God dwells within us. Especially when we enter into peaceful, beautiful, holy places that feel safe, our hearts can settle and naturally rise in openness to the divine and can swell with gratitude for our lives.[15]

---

[15] We can understand why the *General Instruction for the Roman Missal* (*GIRM*) would emphasize the importance of the beauty of the church building right after indicating the importance of the active participation of the faithful in it: "Therefore, churches or other places should be suitable for carrying out the sacred action and for ensuring the active participation of the faithful. Moreover, sacred buildings and requisites for divine worship should be truly worthy and beautiful and be signs and symbols of heavenly realities" (*GIRM* 288).

This can be harder when the environment is chaotic, disorganized, ugly, or marred by a history of violence. Likewise, when events trigger something in us and our nervous systems move into a state of hyperarousal—fight or flight—because of a real or perceived aggressor, it is impossible to settle into silence. In that case, we hear only the pounding of our own hearts until we can recover a sense of safety and are able to ground ourselves.[16]

At times, we avoid silence because, in this interior movement, it can become evident where our attachments lie. When the external occupations cease, thoughts and feelings begin to rise within. These can point to places of pain in our hearts, and the pain can begin to resurface. The thoughts that come up might repeat painful phrases or try to work through difficult and confusing interactions. The less self-reflection we make time for, the more difficult it is for us to track what is happening in our minds and bodies.

The lament of St. Augustine captures this: "Late have I loved Thee, O Beauty so ancient and so new, late have I loved Thee! And behold, Thou wert within and I was without. I was looking for Thee out there, and I threw myself, deformed as I was, upon those well-formed things which Thou hast made. Thou wert with me, yet I was not with Thee. These things held me far from Thee."[17] St. Augustine found himself unable to enter inside himself in silence to meet God within him and continued pushing to the exterior to find God in places that were within his control.

---

[16] For more on trauma and grounding, see Bessel A. Van der Kolk, *The Body Keeps the Score: Brain, Mind, and Body in the Healing of Trauma* (New York: Penguin Books, 2015).

[17] St. Augustine of Hippo, *Confessions*, ed. Roy Joseph Deferrari, trans. Vernon Bourke, vol. 21 of The Fathers of the Church (Washington, DC: Catholic University of America Press, 1953), 297.

Silence can make us feel out of control, as we may face our uncontrollable restlessness or our guilty consciences when we enter into silence. Entering into silence can feel like a stripping away of comforts in a way that confronts us with reality. We face our existential contingency—we cannot sustain ourselves in being by our own power—and the otherness of all things. At the same time, with faith, this can help us to realize that we are willed into being by another, meaning that our lives are a gift, and all other things that exist also have the quality of a gift. We do not have to control them or create them but only receive them from the fullness of God. Pope Benedict XVI described this experience of silence when he spoke at the Carthusian Charterhouse near Rome: "By withdrawing into silence and solitude, human beings, so to speak, 'expose' themselves to reality in their nakedness, to that apparent 'void,'… in order to experience instead Fullness, the presence of God, of the most real Reality that exists and that lies beyond the tangible dimension."[18]

Dr. Conrad Baars, a Catholic psychologist, also describes the way that silence can help to heal the unaffirmed and support everyone in living "the affirming life." The affirming life, in the language of Dr. Baars, is the capacity to respond emotionally to the goodness of reality and to engage the mystery of reality with awe and wonder. For us to live in this way, he counsels restricting the activity of the mind, so often filled with "an abundance of thoughts, judgments, opinions, comparisons, if not prejudgments and a know-it-all-attitude."[19] The overstimulated mind of modern

---

[18] Pope Benedict XVI, Homily for Vespers at the Church of the Charterhouse of Serra San Bruno, October 9, 2011.

[19] Conrad W. Baars, *Feeling and Healing Your Emotions*, ed. Suzanne M. Baars and Bonnie N. Shayne, updated ed. (Alachua, FL: Bridge-Logos, 2009), 166.

man inhibits the potential for awe and wonder and limits our capacity to discover a deeper meaning in the things we have seen many times before:

> His overdeveloped, overstimulated "mind" prevents his "heart" from being present with the awe and wonder of a child who sees a dandelion for the first time; from letting the unknown become part of him, to let the mystery of the unknown be and not demand it to be like the already known. His "mind" prevents his "heart" from being moved with love and joy and tenderness, from being authentically present to the other for the sake of the other.[20]

At the same time, Dr. Baars recognizes that such openness of heart is not easy. In fact, such openness is very vulnerable. If we open our hearts to others, we can easily be hurt. We have learned to close our hearts because of pain from wounds of our past. For this reason, it can be a benefit to practice silence in nature, where our openness of heart is safer:

> The unaffirmed person, therefore, must dare to restrict the activity of his "mind" so his "heart" can be more open and sensitive. It takes courage to be open with the "heart," for one is more vulnerable when one relinquishes the protective workings of the "mind." For this reason the unaffirmed person must first apply these principles only to the world of animals, plants, and minerals—to what we usually call nature. In that world he cannot be hurt as he has been hurt by the human beings who failed to be present to him. For the time being, while engaged in "natural or earthly

---

[20] Ibid.

contemplation" he must try not to "bother" with people, or at least to do so as infrequently as possible.[21]

Discovering the dynamics of the gift of creation is one way to encounter silence. Another is to realize that God wants us to know that He is a Father who loves us, and He gives us permission to view our restlessness in silence like the fidgeting of a little child. Cardinal Sarah describes the childlikeness that can develop in the asceticism of silence: "The asceticism of silence allows a person to enter into the mystery of God by becoming little, like a child.... Silence strips man and makes him like a child: pure but frail, innocent, and without provisions."[22] Our flurry of words and our frenetic activity are defenses that we use to protect ourselves, to shield ourselves from the nakedness that we can feel in silence, but if we can allow ourselves to be held lovingly and patiently by our Heavenly Father, we can learn to settle slowly into the silence.

The good news is that these experiences of our restlessness can alert us to our need for God. Like the thorn in the flesh that St. Paul describes (2 Cor. 12:7–10), our inner reactions to silence can alert us to a greater need for God's grace. And God always desires to provide for us in our need. Behind all our psychological defenses there is something to defend—a vulnerable part of us that is in need of special care. The defenses that are exposed by entering into silence can reveal parts of us that are feeling particularly vulnerable. We can come to discover inner wounds that can become the occasions for grace, as God promised St. Paul: "My grace is sufficient for you, for my power is made perfect in weakness" (2 Cor. 12:9).

---

[21] Ibid., 167.
[22] Sarah and Diat, *The Power of Silence*, nos. 93–94.

The Hidden Power of Silence in the Mass

Bringing all of this together, we can say confidently that silence is important for our spiritual life, for self-knowledge, and for our inner healing. It's no wonder Jesus entered repeatedly into silence, providing an encouraging example for us. And it's no wonder the liturgy also provides spaces of silence for us to enter more deeply into the Sacred Mysteries made present in the words and gestures of the rite.

As mentioned earlier, silence can also have a negative meaning. While some people's defenses include a flurry of words or frenetic activity, others' defenses include shutting down, clamming up, and freezing. In this case, silence can become a kind of hiding place, as Adam found in the garden when he felt shame. Silence can be more oriented to keeping others out than to keeping something precious safe. This leads to the passive-aggressive behavior called the silent treatment, when one person intentionally shuts down another. Here again, it would be unhelpful simply to condemn this behavior in ourselves and more valuable to seek the underlying cause. What vulnerable part of us are we defending by wielding silence in this way?

In the world of social media, this has become known as "ghosting," indicating that a person acts toward another as if he or she has disappeared, by not answering e-mails or messages or any other kind of electronic communication. These are negative experiences of silence, when silence is used as a psychological weapon or as a psychological defense. This is very different from what Jesus was exhorting us to incorporate into our lives: "When you pray, go into your room and shut the door and pray to your Father who is in secret; and your Father who sees in secret will reward you" (Matt. 6:6). Rather than encouraging ghosting, Jesus is inviting us in these words into a safe place of hidden intimacy with Him, where we can receive the love He wants to bring to the littlest and most vulnerable parts of us.

The silence that is prescribed in the liturgy should be viewed in this positive way as creating places of hiddenness that make us secure enough to be vulnerable, like little children, and open to the loving embrace that our Father extends to us. We are stepping away from a flurry of words and activity, often laced with the harshness of this fallen world, in order to hear and savor the words of love that our Father whispers to us as His beloved children. In this way, the liturgy, with its ritual gestures and prescribed silences, provides a kind of veil beneath which we are safe to confront the reality of ourselves in all our strengths and weaknesses and the reality of God in all His love. Romano Guardini describes this beautifully:

> The liturgy is wonderfully reserved. It scarcely expresses, even, certain aspects of spiritual surrender and submission, or else it veils them in such rich imagery that the soul still feels that it is hidden and secure. The prayer of the Church does not probe and lay bare the heart's secrets; it is as restrained in thought as in imagery; it does, it is true, awaken very profound and very tender emotions and impulses, but it leaves them hidden. There are certain feelings of surrender, certain aspects of interior candor that cannot be publicly proclaimed, at any rate in their entirety, without danger to spiritual modesty. The liturgy has perfected a masterly instrument that has made it possible for us to express our inner life in all its fullness and depth, without divulging our secrets—*secretum meum mihi*. We can pour out our hearts and still feel that nothing has been dragged to light that should remain hidden.[23]

---

[23] Romano Guardini, Joseph Ratzinger, and Robert Sarah, *The Spirit of the Liturgy: Commemorative Edition* (San Francisco: Ignatius Press, 2018), 287.

Prescriptions for silence in the Roman Rite

We are realizing more and more clearly that silence is part of the liturgy. We respond, by singing and praying, to the God who addresses us, but the greater mystery, surpassing all words, summons us to silence. It must, of course, be a silence with content, not just the absence of speech and action. We should expect the liturgy to give us a positive stillness that will restore us. Such stillness is not just a pause, in which a thousand thoughts and desires assault us, but a time of recollection, giving us an inward peace, allowing us to draw breath and rediscover the one thing necessary, which we have forgotten. That is why silence cannot be simply "made," organized as if it were one activity among many. It is no accident that, on all sides, people are seeking techniques of meditation, a spirituality for emptying the mind. One of man's deepest needs is making its presence felt, a need that is manifestly not being met in our present form of the liturgy.[24]

Cardinal Ratzinger (who would become Pope Benedict XVI) urged us to revisit the practices of silence in the liturgy. He foresaw the possibilities for inward peace and for rediscovering the primacy of God in our lives. He envisioned this as an antidote to the defection of our Christian faithful to non-Christian forms of meditation that will never meet their deepest need for encounter with Christ. He also recognized that this will not happen by accident or by mechanically following certain procedures. The silence we seek requires the proper disposition of heart coming into encounter with the proper content. Then it acquires real depth for interior transformation.

---

[24] Ibid., 223.

The *General Instruction of the Roman Missal* (GIRM) presents the expectations for silence in the Roman Rite of the Mass. The GIRM establishes that silence is in itself a ritual gesture, and Pope Francis urges us to practice it with utmost care: "We are called to enact with extreme care the symbolic gesture of silence. Through it the Spirit gives us shape, gives us form."[25] The GIRM also explains that silence in the Mass is not a monolithic reality. Rather, there are various ways of praying in the silence of the Mass, depending on the movements of the Mass in which they occur:

> Sacred silence also, as part of the celebration, is to be observed at the designated times [*Sacrosanctum Concilium* 30]. Its nature, however, depends on the moment when it occurs in the different parts of the celebration. For in the Penitential Act and again after the invitation to pray, individuals recollect themselves; whereas after a reading or after the Homily, all meditate briefly on what they have heard; then after Communion, they praise God in their hearts and pray to him. (45)

The GIRM lists several examples of silent moments in the Mass and the different ways in which we should pray during those periods. It does not intend to be comprehensive here, though, and we will identify some additional times and ways of praying in the silence that we will explore throughout this book. Furthermore, we will see that there are various ways in which silence is included in the Mass, so there are various ways to pray in the silence.

How are we to know how to pray in the silences? In some cases, we are directed by the text that precedes the silence, such as, in the Introductory Rites, after the priest invites the faithful

[25] Pope Francis, *Desiderio Desideravi*, no. 52.

to acknowledge their sins or after he announces, "Let us pray." In other cases, when the *GIRM* prescribes that certain ritual actions be carried out in silence, the gestures themselves and even some prayers that the priest is instructed to pray *in secreto*, or "quietly," can guide us in how to pray in these silences.

Before exploring these points more deeply, let us consider the role of silence more generally in the liturgy. Then, in the next section, we will look more closely at the role of the silent prayers of the priest.

Although silence in the liturgy sometimes appears to be, at best, a pause between liturgical movements or, at worst, a mistake or an accidental break in the liturgical action, silence is meant to be a part of the liturgical rite as intentionally as any other word or action. The postconciliar document on music in the liturgy, *Musicam Sacram*, explains:

> At the proper times, all should observe a reverent silence. Through it the faithful are not only not considered as extraneous or dumb spectators at the liturgical service, but are associated more intimately in the mystery that is being celebrated, thanks to that interior disposition which derives from the word of God that they have heard, from the songs and prayers that have been uttered, and from spiritual union with the priest in the parts that he says or sings himself.[26]

The acknowledgment that the faithful are not "extraneous or dumb spectators" and yet are participating interiorly in silence reiterates the goals of the liturgical movement, as explained by Pope Benedict

---

[26] *Musicam Sacram*, in Austin P. Flannery, ed., *Documents of Vatican II* (Grand Rapids, MI: William B. Eerdmans, 1975), 85. Quoted in Sarah, "Silence in the Liturgy."

XVI. In addressing the clergy of Rome just before his resignation of the papal office, Pope Benedict XVI described the rationale of the Second Vatican Council from his privileged vantage point of having been a theological adviser present in the discussions. He explained that in the old rite of the Mass, it was as if there were two parallel liturgies taking place—one liturgy in the pews among the faithful who prayed various devotions and one in the sanctuary with the priest and server carrying out the rituals of the Mass. Simply said, the innovation of the liturgical movement was to unite the two liturgies such that the devotional prayers of the faithful in the pews would be guided by the movements and prayers of the Mass celebrated by the priest and the servers in the sanctuary:

> After the First World War, Central and Western Europe had seen the growth of the liturgical movement, a rediscovery of the richness and depth of the liturgy, which until then had remained, as it were, locked within the priest's Roman Missal, while the people prayed with their own prayer books, prepared in accordance with the heart of the people, seeking to translate the lofty content, the elevated language of classical liturgy into more emotional words, closer to the hearts of the people. But it was as if there were two parallel liturgies: the priest with the altar-servers, who celebrated Mass according to the Missal, and the laity, who prayed during Mass using their own prayer books, at the same time, while knowing substantially what was happening on the altar. But now there was a rediscovery of the beauty, the profundity, the historical, human, and spiritual riches of the Missal, and it became clear that it should not be merely a representative of the people, a young altar-server, saying "*Et cum spiritu tuo*," and so on, but that there should truly

be a dialogue between priest and people: truly the liturgy of the altar and the liturgy of the people should form one single liturgy, an active participation, such that the riches reach the people. And in this way, the liturgy was rediscovered and renewed.[27]

One basic way in which the prayers of the faithful in the pews are synchronized and guided by the prayers of the priest and the servers in the sanctuary is through dialogical responses, with the people taking up the words that were previously spoken only by the servers, such as "And with your spirit." The Second Vatican Council intended more than merely external participation, however. Clearly, the faithful say only a few of the words in the Mass; the majority of their participation takes place without words. Furthermore, the faithful need to learn how to participate not only when the priest is the only one speaking but even when no one is speaking or singing. In order for the prayers of the faithful in the pews to be coordinated with the ritual movements of the priest and the servers in the sanctuary, it is necessary to coordinate their hearts with the ritual gestures that are not accompanied by words. For example, one significant part of the Mass in which few or even no words are spoken by the faithful, and yet their participation is of the utmost importance, is the Offertory, when they, too, are expected to offer themselves:

> The Church, therefore, earnestly desires that Christ's faithful, when present at this mystery of faith, should not be there as strangers or silent spectators; on the contrary, through a good understanding of the rites and prayers they

[27] Pope Benedict XVI, Address to the Parish Priests and the Clergy of Rome, February 14, 2013.

should take part in the sacred action conscious of what they are doing, with devotion and full collaboration.... By offering the Immaculate Victim, not only through the hands of the priest, but also with him, they should learn also to offer themselves.[28]

In order for the faithful to enter into this central point in the liturgy, they must learn how to participate in the silence of the Mass. We can see how this emerges clearly from the conciliar and postconciliar teaching. It is understandable, then, why the papal master of ceremonies under Pope Benedict XVI and in the first years of the pontificate of Pope Francis would write the following about the liturgical moments of silence in the Mass:

This silence is not synonymous with idleness or a lack of participation. Its purpose is to make all the faithful enter into the act of love by which Jesus offers himself to the Father on the cross for the salvation of the world. This truly sacred silence is the liturgical moment during which it is necessary to say yes, with all our strength, to Christ's action, so that it might become our action too in everyday life.[29]

We can understand, further, why Cardinal Robert Sarah, then-prefect of the Congregation for Divine Worship and the Discipline of the Sacraments, emphasized the place of silence, as foreseen

---

[28] Second Vatican Council, Constitution on the Sacred Liturgy *Sacrosanctum Concilium* (December 4, 1963), no. 48.

[29] Msgr. Guido Marini, *La Liturgie: Gloire de Dieu, sanctification de l'homme* (Perpignan: Artège, 2013), 71–72; quoted in Cardinal Robert Sarah, "Silence in the Liturgy," trans. Michael J. Miller, *Catholic World Report*, February 10, 2016, https://www.catholic worldreport.com/2016/02/10/silence-in-the-liturgy.

in the guidelines of the Second Vatican Council's reform of the Roman Rite, and quoted from Cardinal Ratzinger about the full, conscious, and active participation that takes place in silence:

> Silence is therefore not at all absent from the Ordinary Form of the Roman Rite, at least if we follow its guidelines and celebrate in the spirit of its recommendations. Unfortunately, too often "it was forgotten that the Council also included silence under *actuosa participatio*, for silence facilitates a really deep, personal participation, allowing us to listen inwardly to the Lord's word. Many liturgies now lack all trace of this silence."[30]

A decade after this statement from Cardinal Ratzinger, Pope St. John Paul II addressed bishops from the United States on an *ad limina* visit and offered deeper reflections on the same points. He emphasized that silence is not passive but is truly active participation, even profoundly active. Listening requires effort and attention, and this is a discipline that must be learned. Furthermore, this silence has a truly countercultural quality. That means that it is something that must be cultivated in the liturgy because it will not naturally come into the liturgy from the (noisy) culture of the world:

> Active participation certainly means that, in gesture, word, song and service, all the members of the community take part in an act of worship, which is anything but inert or passive. Yet active participation does not preclude the active passivity of silence, stillness and listening: indeed,

---

[30] Sarah, "Silence in the Liturgy," quoting Joseph Cardinal Ratzinger, with Vittorio Messori, *The Ratzinger Report: An Exclusive Interview on the State of the Church* (San Francisco: Ignatius Press, 1985), 127.

it demands it. Worshippers are not passive, for instance, when listening to the readings or the homily, or following the prayers of the celebrant, and the chants and music of the liturgy. These are experiences of silence and stillness, but they are in their own way profoundly active. In a culture which neither favors nor fosters meditative quiet, the art of interior listening is learned only with difficulty. Here we see how the liturgy, though it must always be properly inculturated, must also be counter-cultural.[31]

Pope Francis likewise insists on the absolute importance of silence in the liturgy: "Among the ritual acts that belong to the whole assembly, silence occupies a place of absolute importance. Many times it is expressly prescribed in the rubrics."[32] He further establishes the importance of interior participation in the liturgy, noting that without this, even celebrating the ritual with utter fidelity would not be enough for full participation:

Let us be clear here: every aspect of the celebration must be carefully tended to (space, time, gestures, words, objects, vestments, song, music …) and every rubric must be observed. Such attention would be enough to prevent robbing from the assembly what is owed to it; namely, the paschal mystery celebrated according to the ritual that the Church sets down. But even if the quality and the proper action of the celebration were guaranteed, that would not be enough to make our participation full.[33]

---

[31] Pope St. John Paul II, Address to the Bishops of the Episcopal Conference of the United States of America (Washington, Oregon, Idaho, Montana, and Alaska), October 9, 1998.

[32] Pope Francis, *Desiderio Desideravi* 52.

[33] Ibid., no. 23.

Lastly, we draw some guidance from the *General Instruction on the Liturgy of the Hours* (GILH), which lists points in the Liturgy of the Hours when silence could be fruitful. Unlike in the Mass, these silences are all of the same kind—namely, the silence of savoring the encounter:

> In order to receive in our hearts the full sound of the voice of the Holy Spirit and to unite our personal prayer more closely with the word of God and the public voice of the Church, it is permissible, as occasion offers and prudence suggests, to have an interval of silence. It may come either after the repetition of the antiphon at the end of the psalm, in the traditional way, especially if the psalm-prayer is to be said after the pause (see no. 112), or after the short or longer readings, either before or after the responsory. (202a)

The *GILH* also suggests that there is a positive way and a negative way to include silence in the liturgy: "Care must be taken to avoid the kind of silence that would disturb the structure of the office or annoy and weary those taking part" (202b). Just as silence in personal life can be either positive (as a way of being stripped and becoming more vulnerable and open to new encounters) or negative (as a way of shutting down, hiding, or giving the silent treatment), so we can see silence functioning positively or negatively in the liturgy. Neither absolute silence nor endless words are desirable, then, but a balance, or what Pope Benedict XVI called an "eco-system": "It is necessary to develop an appropriate environment, a kind of 'eco-system' that maintains a just equilibrium between silence, words, images and sounds."[34]

---

[34] Pope Benedict XVI, Message for the Forty-Sixth World Day of Communication: Silence and Word: Path of Evangelization, January 24, 2012.

The secret prayers of the priest

The Roman Ritual for the Mass instructs the priest to offer certain prayers quietly (*secreto*).[35] These "private" prayers of the priest in the celebration of the Holy Mass carry layers of meaning. Both priest and laypeople benefit from some mystagogical reflection on these prayers—first, reflection on the importance of reciting prescribed yet unheard prayers and then specific reflections on the words, gestures, and context of the Mass for each of the prayers.

Therefore, silence in the Mass carries a meaning of a shared hidden fullness with God, a form of divine communion and intimacy. It is intended in the same spirit as Jesus' exhortation for us to go into our inner room and pray to the Father in secret, and the Father, who sees in secret, will reward us. Some might interpret Jesus' words as referring only to the need for private prayer outside of the public worship of liturgical prayer. The intentional silences in the Mass and the unheard prayers of the priest, however, are intended to overcome that false dichotomy, and they point out the way that our secret prayer is also supposed to permeate the Mass. This is the sign value of seeing the priest's lips move silently or possibly hearing only his whispering as he addresses his secret prayer to the Father. Thus, the very fact that the prayers are intended *not* to be heard is an important ritual action in the Mass.

Each of these prayers, then, is a sign of the secret inner dialogue that takes place between God and each believer during the Mass,

---

[35] This section and the other sections containing reflections on the silent prayers of the priest in the Mass were published earlier in a modified form in Boniface Hicks, "The Quiet That Speaks—The Silent Prayers of the Priest at Mass," *Adoremus* (blog), July 15, 2021, https://adoremus.org/2021/07/the-quiet-that-speaks-the-silent-prayers-of-the-priest-at-mass/. They are reprinted in this book with permission.

and each is also specifically a sign that the priest himself has a personal inner dialogue with God during the Mass. The priest is not merely a functionary who mechanically carries out certain ritual words and gestures in order to bring about a particular result, however powerful and important that result may be. He is also personally a participant in these sacred mysteries. His own relationship with God grows through his silent, internal participation in the prayers of the Mass, as Cardinal Ratzinger notes: "The silent prayers of the priest invite him to make his task truly personal, so that he may give his whole self to the Lord. They highlight the way in which all of us, each one personally yet together with everyone else, have to approach the Lord."[36]

The priest plays a role for the sake of the faithful, and he also participates in the Mass on his own behalf, as Cardinal Ratzinger explains: "The priest presides over an encounter with the living God and as a person who is on his way to God."[37] That comes through especially clearly in the conclusion of the Preparation of the Gifts, in which several of the silent prayers are prescribed. After silently (or mostly silently) preparing the altar, the priest says, "Pray, brethren, that my sacrifice and yours …" Here we see that there are two ways of offering this sacrifice (mine and yours) because the priest plays a different role from that of the faithful (distinctly offering the sacrifice of Christ in a way the faithful do not), and yet because of the silent prayers he has been addressing to God personally while preparing the gifts, we see that he also has his own personal participation, similar to the rest of the faithful.

Obviously, there is nothing secret about the content of the prayers spoken quietly (*in secreto*) by the priest. They are easily

---

[36] Guardini, Ratzinger, and Sarah, *The Spirit of the Liturgy*, 227.
[37] Ibid., 226.

accessible and published in the vernacular for all to find. They are also meant not to exhaust the inner prayer of the priest but to serve as initial liturgical formulations that help him to enter into and offer himself more fully at those points in the liturgy and to provide starting points for the personal prayer of the lay faithful at those points. "The celebrant's silence and his gestures of piety move the faithful who are participating in the celebration to be conscious of the need to prepare themselves, to convert, given the importance of the liturgical moment in which they are taking part: before the reading of the Gospel, or at the beginning of the Eucharistic Prayer."[38]

We will consider each of the silent prayers of the priest as we consider each of the silent parts of the Mass. These prayers provide important insights for understanding the texture of these parts of the Mass and help to guide the prayer of the faithful in these silences.

Learning silence in prayer

Mary's example

Mary's silence makes her the perfect receptacle for the Divine Word. When she is presented to us at the Annunciation (Luke 1:26–38), she is in a posture to receive the message from the archangel. She has the ears to hear what he comes to tell her. Artists and mystics have envisioned her in a posture of openness even before the message. As the Immaculate Conception, she does not have to contend with the same interior disintegration that is a challenge for us. Our interior disintegration, manifested in inner conflicts, endless mental chatter, defensive comparisons, and

---

[38] See Fr. Mauro Gagliardi, "A Silence That Contemplates and Adores," EWTN, https://www.ewtn.com/catholicism/library/silence-that-contemplates-and-adores-5001.

countless judgments, continually interferes with our capacity to receive the fullness of the Word. Our Lady does not have such interior noise because, having been preserved from Original Sin, her nature is already perfected by grace.[39]

We can consider the shape of this interior stillness in the Immaculate Heart of Mary—indeed, even in the whole body and especially in the womb of Mary—prior to the Annunciation. Her body is a silent vessel, perfectly ready to receive the Word of God. As the Maronite Offertory hymn acclaims, her womb is good earth: "Of the Virgin Mary I was born, taking flesh as man; as good earth receives a seed, her womb received me."[40]

Caryll Houselander reflected poetically on a particular emptiness of Mary that is not merely a useless space but a particular "shape," ready to be filled, like a reed or a cup or a nest:

> It is not a formless emptiness, a void without meaning; on the contrary it has a shape, a form given to it by the purpose for which it is intended. It is emptiness like the hollow in the reed, the narrow riftless emptiness, which can have only one destiny: to receive the piper's breath and to utter the song that is in his heart. It is emptiness like the hollow in the cup, shaped to receive water or wine. It is emptiness like that of the bird's nest, built in a round warm ring to receive the little bird. The pre-Advent emptiness of Our Lady's

---

[39] The name with which the angel greets Mary, *kecharitomene*, is the strongest biblical witness of the dogma of the Immaculate Conception. This name spoken by the angel never occurs outside of this instance in all of Greek literature, and it means "fully transformed by grace." See Ignace de la Potterie and Bertrand Buby, *Mary in the Mystery of the Covenant* (New York: Alba House, 1992).

[40] Maronite liturgy *Book of Offering* (2012), 750.

purposeful virginity was indeed like those three things. She was a reed through which the Eternal Love was to be piped as a shepherd's song. She was the flowerlike chalice into which the purest water of humanity was to be poured, mingled with wine, changed to the crimson blood of love, and lifted up in sacrifice. She was the warm nest rounded to the shape of humanity to receive the Divine Little Bird.[41]

Mary invites us by her example to consider the shape of our own interiority. Her womb and her heart are perfectly shaped to receive the entire Word of God. What does it look like inside my heart? Is there room for Him? What song can He play through the space in my heart? What precious offering can He pour into the chalice of my heart? What new life can be born in the nest of my heart?

Through Baptism, each of us has been given the capacity to bear Christ and, by grace, even to become one with Him. Although we struggle and suffer with disintegration, we are made for divine union. Even when it seems that the ravages of our sins or the wounds we bear from the sins of others would prevent us from receiving Him, we can remember the moving words of Pope St. John Paul II: "*We are not the sum of our weaknesses and failures; we are the sum of the Father's love for us and our real capacity to become the image of his Son.*"[42]

Learning from St. Benedict

St. Benedict spent three years in solitude in a cave in Subiaco before founding a dozen monasteries in that valley. That time in

---

[41] Caryll Houselander, *The Reed of God* (Notre Dame, IN: Christian Classics, 2006), 7–8.

[42] Pope St. John Paul II, Homily at the Closing Mass of the Seventeenth World Youth Day, in Toronto, Canada, July 28, 2002.

silence for him was formative. Although he also received God's love through the daily charity of the monk Romanus, who brought him a portion of his own bread, St. Benedict primarily learned to receive God's love through extensive periods of silence. In his Rule, he incorporated silence in ways that can be instructive for us. In regard to silence in prayer, we can see the importance that St. Benedict places on silence in the oratory, the place of prayer:

> After the Work of God,[43] all should leave in complete silence and with reverence for God, so that a brother who may wish to pray alone will not be disturbed by the insensitivity of another. Moreover, if at other times someone chooses to pray privately, he may simply go in and pray, not in a loud voice, but with tears and heartfelt devotion. Accordingly, anyone who does not pray in this manner is not to remain in the oratory after the Work of God, as we have said; then he will not interfere with anyone else.[44]

In this passage of the Holy Rule, St. Benedict provides a simple teaching on prayer: that it should be in complete silence and with reverence for God. This is not a stoic silence; St. Benedict advocates that it be filled with "heartfelt devotion" and even tears. At the same time, these are not loud cries and tears but, rather, a reverent, silent prayer that "will not interfere with anyone else." St. Benedict was a master of silence, and he can be a good teacher for us if we let him.

---

[43] In his Rule, St. Benedict refers to the Liturgy of the Hours as the "Work of God" because it is the monks' primary work for God and because God is at work in the monks' liturgical prayer.

[44] St. Benedict, *RB 1980: The Rule of St. Benedict in Latin and English with Notes*, ed. Timothy Fry (Collegeville, MN: Liturgical Press, 1981), 52:2–5. Hereafter this will be cited as *RB*.

Practicing silence in prayer

Entering into deeper silence is important for the growth of any-one's prayer life. Here are a few simple steps to get you started. In time, these steps will integrate organically into your prayer life and will become second nature, but at first, you may need to be more intentional in practicing them. It may be helpful to precede these steps with the preparation steps that we will consider in the next chapter, but for now, just try this silent visualization exercise.

First, close your eyes and imagine our loving God sitting in front of you. You may picture Him as a Father, or you may visualize Jesus, the Son of God, according to the most beautiful, moving pictures of Him you have seen. When you picture Him, try to see His mercy, gentleness, and tenderness. Furthermore, consider that He has been eagerly awaiting you. He was thinking of you, loving you, even thirsting for you before you even thought about praying. Try to sit with Him for a minute in silence, just letting Him look at you and love you. Is there anything He wants to say to you? You can ask Him. Is there anything you want to say to Him? You can tell Him. Try to extend this time with Him in silent prayer. If a minute is comfortable, extend it to two minutes or five minutes or ten minutes. It is not necessary to come up with words. It's good simply to be with Him.

If you have trouble with this exercise, there is no shame in that. There are many things that can make this exercise difficult. Try to notice what is interfering with your visualization or what is distracting you, and perhaps write it down. It may be a matter of settling your heart, which will be presented at the end of the next chapter. In that case, simply keep reading and revisit this exercise after practicing the preparation steps at the end of chapter 2. If you have a hard time visualizing a Father who loves you or visualizing Jesus loving you, try to be compassionate with yourself. What is the image that comes to you? Depending on our experiences, our images of God may become distorted. In that case, perhaps just placing yourself in the presence of the Holy Spirit will help. The Holy Spirit is an embrace of love. You can let yourself settle into that loving embrace, which is divine.

Practicing silence takes time and patience. If you were successful with this exercise, try to repeat it regularly in your prayer. If you are already integrating this kind of silence into your prayer, try to bring it into the Mass. Take time before, during, and after Mass to practice silent prayer. Let yourself rest in the presence of our God, who loves you so much.

Try it!

Find as silent a place as you can (in your house, in church, or elsewhere) and spend ten minutes in silence. What comes up inside of you? What do you feel? Are there words that come to you? Does spending time in silence feel good, such that you want to extend the time? Is it challenging for you so that you want to quit? Try to describe your experience.

For further reflection

✝ Where is the most physically silent place in your life? What has been your experience of physical silence? What has been your experience of inner silence or personal silence? How do you make time for silence in prayer, and how might you extend that time?

✝ What has been your experience of silence in prayer in general and in the Mass in particular? In this chapter, we considered the Church's many guidelines for silence in the Mass. Discuss the guidelines you found most surprising. For most of the Mass, the congregation is not speaking or singing. Explain how this personal silence can still be an active participation.

✝ Silence seems to be the same as inactivity, but that's not necessarily true. Explain how silence can go well with and even be a necessary precursor to active participation in the Mass. How can it associate us more intimately with the mystery?

✝ What makes it hard to maintain silence in your heart? Explain how the overstimulation of your mind can keep you from entering into your heart. What are some ways that you have found helpful for settling your mind and entering into your heart?

✝ Not all silence is the same. In what ways can silence have a negative meaning? Recall any times in which you have been hurt by silence (the silent treatment, secrets, etc.). Recall any times in which you have been scared by silence (a house that is too quiet, a lack of response from someone).

2

Preparing for Mass (Ascetical)

*The ears of all the people were attentive to
the book of the law.... All the people wept when
they heard the words of the law. (Neh. 8:3, 9)*

Even before there is something to listen to or the possibility of an encounter, we must learn to cultivate silence in our hearts. This is essential for understanding ourselves and preparing ourselves for what we will hear. Furthermore, this preparation enables our responses to come from a deeper place in us and not simply be rote reactions, as Pope Benedict XVI expressed in his 2012 message for the World Day of Communications: "In silence, we are better able to listen to and understand ourselves; ideas come to birth and acquire depth; we understand with greater clarity what it is we want to say and what we expect from others; and we choose how to express ourselves."[45]

Pope Francis teaches us that the first movement in the liturgy is the silence of preparation, and he describes it eloquently as the very context of the whole liturgy: "The entire Eucharistic celebration is

---

[45] Pope Benedict XVI, Message for the Forty-Sixth World Day of Communication.

immersed in the silence which precedes its beginning and which marks every moment of its ritual unfolding."[46]

The silence of preparation begins before Mass and continues into the Introductory Rites. The *Catechism of the Catholic Church* tells us that this should begin as we enter the church and that the building itself should facilitate this kind of preparation: "A church must also be a space that invites us to the recollection and silent prayer that extend and internalize the great prayer of the Eucharist" (CCC 1185). Pope Benedict XVI helps us understand the complementarity between beauty and silence and notes how the two are regularly brought together for the sake of fostering contemplation:

> In every age, men and women who have consecrated their lives to God in prayer—like monks and nuns—have founded their communities in particularly beautiful places: in the countryside, on hilltops, in mountain valleys, on the shores of lakes or of the sea and even on small islands. These places combine two very important elements for contemplative life: the beauty of creation, which evokes the beauty of the Creator, and silence, which is guaranteed by living far from cities and the great thoroughfares of the media.... The silence and beauty of the place in which the monastic community dwells—a simple and austere beauty—are like a reflection of the spiritual harmony which the community itself seeks to create.[47]

This is also important for the priests and the ministers as they prepare for the celebration of the Mass, as the *GIRM* states: "Even

---

[46] Pope Francis, *Desiderio Desideravi* 52.

[47] Pope Benedict XVI, General Audience, catechesis on prayer, August 10, 2011.

before the celebration itself, it is a praiseworthy practice for silence to be observed in the church, in the sacristy, in the vesting room, and in adjacent areas, so that all may dispose themselves to carry out the sacred celebration in a devout and fitting manner" (45). The *GIRM* is confident that the best way to prepare for a devout celebration is through silence. This will not happen, however, if the silence is merely a lack of exterior noise. We must also take positive steps to use the silence well for interior preparation. A physically silent sacristy full of people texting on their cell phones is certainly not what the *GIRM* has in mind.

Furthermore, the Introductory Rites of the Mass are arranged, in part, to facilitate this kind of interior preparation: "Their purpose is to ensure that the faithful, who come together as one, establish communion and dispose themselves properly to listen to the Word of God and to celebrate the Eucharist worthily" (*GIRM* 46). Correspondingly, there are two periods of silence prescribed in these Introductory Rites.

The first is after the priest's invitation: "Brothers and sisters, let us acknowledge our sins, and so prepare ourselves to celebrate the sacred mysteries." This provides some space to clear out some of the things that may be weighing us down and to set aside any feelings, thoughts, memories, or images that might interfere with our reception of the Sacred Mysteries. This happens not by compulsion or suppression but by bringing these things into contact with divine mercy; this is precisely what happens as the priest prays: "May Almighty God have mercy on us, forgive us our sins, and bring us to everlasting life."

The second is after the priest says, "Let us pray." Here the Roman Missal (no. 54) prescribes a brief period of silence, for two reasons. The first is for the faithful to become aware of being in God's presence. This is part of the preparatory silence that we are reflecting on in this chapter. The second reason is for the faithful to call to mind their intentions. In chapter 4, we will focus on silence as offering, but we can also note that the offering here can be part of the preparation. Rather than merely clearing out distractions or cleansing them through mercy, we can also offer them up to the Father as part of our prayer. We can toss them into this period of silence and let the priest offer our and everyone's intentions to the Father through the Opening Prayer, called the Collect:

> Truly, there is "a time to be silent, and a time to speak" (Eccles. 3:7), and the Opening Prayer is both. In silence, our prayers well up from our hearts and come to the forefront of our minds. Then, in the words of the Church, the priest gathers these prayers and offers them to the Father, through the Son, in the Holy Spirit. If God thirsts for us so that we might thirst for Him, the Opening Prayer satisfies God's thirst by quenching ours.[48]

We can call this initial silence of preparation an *ascetical silence*, in which we set aside other things—certainly we should set aside bad things but even good things as well—in order to make space for the mysteries we are about to receive. This is the silence that corresponds with listening, as we will discuss in the next chapter: "Silence is above all the positive attitude of someone who prepares to welcome God by listening."[49] In order to listen to someone else, we need to stop talking—both the external chatter and the internal chatter. The stopping is an act of asceticism.

---

[48] Christopher Carstens, *A Devotional Journey into the Mass: How Mass Can Become a Time of Grace, Nourishment, and Devotion* (Manchester, NH: Sophia Institute Press, 2017), 31.
[49] Sarah, "Silence in the Liturgy," 143.

Cardinal Robert Sarah provides a challenging image of this constant noise to which we have become accustomed and acknowledges how difficult it can be to step aside from it. This first step of ascetical silence is not at all easy:

> Without noise, postmodern man falls into a dull, insistent uneasiness. He is accustomed to permanent background noise, which sickens yet reassures him. Without noise, man is feverish, lost. Noise gives him security, like a drug on which he has become dependent. With its festive appearance, noise is a whirlwind that avoids facing itself. Agitation becomes a tranquilizer, a sedative, a morphine pump, a sort of reverie, an incoherent dream-world. But this noise is a dangerous, deceptive medicine, a diabolic lie that helps man avoid confronting himself in his interior emptiness. The awakening will necessarily be brutal.[50]

This is the preparation that the children of Israel made before hearing the law, as documented in Nehemiah 8:1–12. The law had been lost to them, and after Hilkiah found it in the house of the Lord, he read it to the king (2 Kings 22:8), and then Ezra the priest read it to the whole people (Neh. 8:1). The people knew that this law contained the revelation of God. Although God had not revealed His innermost secret to them yet, He had revealed His heart to them in a partial way through this revelation to Moses on Mount Sinai. Before the reading of the law, the people set aside other things and prepared to listen: "The ears of all the people were attentive to the book of the law" (Neh. 8:3). Furthermore, we know they became truly vulnerable and open to what they would

---

[50] Sarah and Diat, *The Power of Silence*, no. 21.

hear because they were moved to tears: "All the people wept when they heard the words of the law" (Neh. 8:9).

Images for reducing distractions

There are various images we can use to visualize this process of preparation for vulnerable listening. In this section, we will focus on the dimension of reducing distractions. In the next section, we will focus on increasing vulnerability.

Making room for God within us

In describing our preparation for listening, Pope Benedict XVI uses the image of creating space: "By remaining silent we allow the other person to speak, to express him or herself; and we avoid being tied simply to our own words and ideas without them being adequately tested. In this way, space is created for mutual listening, and deeper human relationships become possible."[51] Ascetical silence involves cleaning up and clearing out in order to make room. We can think of our interior as a kind of chamber. Scripture speaks of the human person as being a temple of God or a temple of the Holy Spirit (1 Cor. 3:17; 6:19). The *Catechism* speaks of the heart as a place in this way: "The heart is the dwelling-place where I am, where I live; according to the Semitic or Biblical expression, the heart is the place 'to which I withdraw'" (2563). In another passage, the *Catechism* speaks of the heart as the dwelling place of the Lord and compares entering into the church for the Eucharistic liturgy as analogous to entering into the heart in contemplative prayer to be in the presence of God:

> *Entering into contemplative prayer* is like entering into the Eucharistic liturgy: we "gather up" the heart, recollect our whole being

---

[51] Pope Benedict XVI, "Word and Silence."

under the prompting of the Holy Spirit, abide in the dwelling place of the Lord which we are, awaken our faith in order to enter into the presence of him who awaits us (2711).

In this image, our initial interior work in our preparatory, ascetical silence is to order our interior, clean up our inner room, throw out or put away what is unnecessary, and make room for the Lord. This will require, first, taking stock of what is there. When we enter the church and kneel in a pew in silence, what starts coming up in our hearts? The first step is merely to acknowledge what we are feeling and thinking in that moment, without judgment but with simple curiosity. A couple of deep breaths can also help by settling our nervous systems, in case they are keyed up from whatever we have just been involved in. Then we can begin to sort out whatever is coming up. If it is a task that is due or something of that nature, it might be helpful to write a note for ourselves so that we can forget it for now and come back to it later; it is not more important than the Mass we are preparing for. For other things, such as difficult feelings of sadness, hurt, or shame, we can touch them gently by feeling them and holding them out to the Lord or placing them on the altar. There is a reason we are feeling those things. We do not necessarily need to figure that out right away, but we should not suppress those feelings either. We can simply set them aside, just as we might need to set aside a difficult encounter as we begin a meeting with a person. In these ways, we can bring a little order to our inner rooms, to our hearts. This helps to make room for the Lord and all that He wants to communicate to us.

Stretching open

Another image for the ascetical silence that prepares us for receiving the Word at Mass is "paying attention," which we can understand as "stretching open." We hear the word *tension* in *attention*. In both words, we see the ancient, Indo-European particle *ten*, which means "to stretch."[52] This is what we do when we pay attention. We stretch open our hearts to make more room to receive. We are preparing for listening, and so we start paying attention. When we listen attentively, we feel the internal stretching. It takes effort to listen, to try to understand, to open up a space inside ourselves to receive something new. We can understand how Pope Francis can describe it as a kind of martyrdom and a great grace:

> Listening is never easy. Many times it is easier to play deaf. Listening means paying attention, wanting to understand, to value, to respect and to ponder what the other person says. It involves a sort of martyrdom or self-sacrifice, as we try to imitate Moses before the burning bush: we have to remove our sandals when standing on the "holy ground" of our encounter with the one who speaks to me (cf. Ex 3:5). Knowing how to listen is an immense grace, it is a gift which we need to ask for and then make every effort to practice.[53]

Pope Francis offers the helpful image of Moses standing on the "holy ground" before the burning bush to describe the reverence we should have even in human communication. How much more should we stretch our hearts in reverence when we are in the sacramental presence of God in the liturgy?

What interferes with this? Just as in human listening, when we feel that the other has nothing to offer us, we might close down

---

52 *Online Etymology Dictionary*, s.v. "*ten-*," https://www.etymonline.com/word/*ten-.

53 Pope Francis, Message for the Fiftieth World Day of Communication on Communication and Mercy: A Fruitful Encounter, January 24, 2016.

interiorly. If we think we already know what is going to be said, we might mentally check out. If we think what is going to be said is unimportant or uninteresting, we might close up and move our attention elsewhere. Sometimes our internal speed for information consumption is set at such a high rate—especially if we are coming from a more frenetic activity—that we need to slow ourselves down interiorly. In such a case, God can act like a shy child who does not want to share His treasures with someone who is too rushed or too brash to receive them. Thus, we need to stretch to hold ourselves in attention before the mysteries and be ready to receive what God wants to give us. We need to stretch our hearts and slow down to prepare for this kind of listening.

Settling a snow globe

Another image we can use to describe this process of preparing our hearts, in the silence before Mass, to see and hear the Lord is the settling of a snow globe. Shaking the snow globe stirs up the little white flakes so that they obscure the scene inside until they slowly settle back to the bottom. Like the flakes, the many whirling things, including thoughts and feelings, that swirl around within us obscure the presence of God. There is no way simply to stop all the things that are moving around in us. The only way is to hold the snow globe still and let it settle. Trying to shake it in order to speed up the process will only make it worse.

This analogy guides us in a basic movement of preparing our hearts, which is simply to settle ourselves down and give some time and space for the natural process of stilling our interior to take place. It requires patience. Trying to explore and follow up on every thought or feeling would be analogous to shaking the snow globe. Trying to stop certain thoughts or feelings could likewise be a way of stirring them up even more. Although it can be tempting to fix it, it will end up more often like whack-a-mole, and we will be worse off than before.

Like the process of cleaning up and making a space, this process requires a nonjudgmental stance toward our interior. We cannot judge whether the little white flakes should be there—we must simply acknowledge that they *are* there and then patiently let them settle. This initial process of letting our interior noise settle down may need to precede any process of ordering or clearing out our interior. After the initial trivial things settle, we can focus some attention on the more important things that remain.

Images for vulnerability

In addition to the work of removing distractions through clearing our minds, stretching our attention, and patiently letting our interiors settle down, there is a work of cultivating vulnerability. It is one thing to empty a room of clutter; it is another to prepare the room with care for the hospitable reception of guests. This transforms a cold, empty space into a warm, safe chamber for intimate communion. There are several ways to do this, and we can consider several images that can help to cultivate such a vulnerable openness. When we have prepared our hearts well, our encounter with the Lord in that silent interior place will be filled with awe and wonder.

The Italian Montessorian Sofia Cavalletti followed this logic when preparing a place for children to grow in the mysteries of our Catholic Faith. In her Montessori-based program for the religious formation of children, Catechesis of the Good Shepherd, the parish must prepare a special place called an "atrium" where children can encounter and work with the sacred mysteries of the Faith. The atrium uses the best materials—handmade and properly ordered and organized—so that the room contains many secrets for the children to discover with the help of a catechist. The atrium is a beautiful image for the kind of interior ordering and attention that each of us should prepare in our heart, as was discussed in the previous section.

The catechist accompanies the children by presenting the mysteries as the children are ready for them. The catechist is formed to ask pondering questions to help the children open places in their hearts where the mysteries can be received with love. For example, when presenting the parable of the Good Shepherd, the catechist might ask, "Who do you think the sheep are, that the shepherd would know them by name?" This form of catechesis prepares children's hearts to be open to an encounter, helping them to seek answers in their hearts so that they can each have the joy of discovery in awe and wonder. We will explore the experience of awe and wonder more fully in the next chapter, when we reflect on the silence of encounter, but it is worth mentioning here in regard to the preparatory steps that accompany it.[54]

There are several ways in which we can cultivate vulnerability and prepare ourselves for the encounter in silence that brings forth awe and wonder. One is to connect with our littleness before God. Another is to enter into the strange and wonderful world of the Mass by leaning into the adventure that comes with a change in language and symbols.

Becoming like a child

In various ways, we prepare for the Mass by becoming more vulnerable—or we could say more humble. If we come to the Mass

---

[54] For more on the rationale for Catechesis of the Good Shepherd, see Sofia Cavalletti, *The Religious Potential of the Child: Experiencing Scripture and Liturgy with Young Children*, 3rd ed. (Chicago: Liturgy Training Publications, 2020).

already convinced that we know everything and have no needs, we will not be able to receive anything. In vulnerability, we open up our needs. In humility, we acknowledge our limitations. One way to describe this is that we become more childlike; or, to say it another way, we connect with a part of us that is most child-like, which is that part of us that longs for a father or is eager to learn. That inner child might also be a part of us that carries a burden or feels wounded. Sometimes there are parts of us that feel misunderstood, overlooked, or undervalued. Other parts can feel worthless or lost. These are good places to connect to and activate while praying in the silence of the Mass.[55]

How do we do this? We can consider two approaches. One is to connect with our littleness, and the other is to remember the qualities of God. Many people have a sense of what it feels like to be little, to be a child. They can connect with playfulness or childlike trust. They can connect with purity and openness to experience. They can connect with physical smallness and the comfort of being held and cared for. In some cases, this image of our inner child is a representation that comes from a photograph of ourselves when we were little. In a trauma-healing retreat called Grief to Grace, participants are asked to draw a picture of themselves as a little child from before the trauma. In another case, we might connect with an inner child through a vision of our own children or the children around us. I remember seeing a little child crawling on the kneeler in church during Mass and spontaneously feeling the innocence, safety, freedom, and sense of discovery that it brought up in my heart.

---

[55] For more on understanding the dynamics of the inner child, psychological models of subpersonalities, and parts work, see Gerry Ken Crete, *Litanies of the Heart: Relieving Post-Traumatic Stress and Calming Anxiety through Healing Our Parts* (Manchester, NH: Sophia Institute Press, 2024).

Remembering whom we are meeting

Another way to access a childlike part in our hearts is through imagining the God we are preparing to meet. Different parts in us tend to come up as we encounter different persons. We can reflect on the difference in our inner experience when we interact with a powerful person, such as a politician or a pope, as opposed to interacting with a small child or an old woman in a wheelchair. We thus activate different parts of us depending on whom we are expecting to encounter. When we imagine Christ as the Good Shepherd, who seeks us out when we feel most lost, or as the friend who truly understands us, it will open up different parts of us.

Dr. Gerry Crete's doctoral research identified eight ways in which Christ interacts with us:

1. *The Lover*, who loves us with gentleness and humility
2. *The Seeker*, who seeks us with confidence and is attuned to the will of God
3. *The Protector*, who empathizes, rejoices, and prepares a safe place for us
4. *The True Friend*, who knows and affirms us
5. *The Healer*, who relieves our burdens
6. *The Pathfinder*, who calls us to righteousness and holiness
7. *The Bridge Builder*, who calls us to communion with each other, with God, and with others
8. *The Nurturer*, who feeds, nourishes, and calls us to alertness and action[56]

Each of these images helps us to encounter a unique aspect of Christ and to relate our interior experiences to Him. It would be a fruitful exercise to practice calling these images to mind in our

---

[56] See Crete, *Litanies of the Heart*, chap. 3.

private prayer and even in our participation in the Eucharist so as to engage different aspects of Christ and to open up different aspects of our interior experience.

Entering another world

Another way to prepare ourselves to encounter Christ is by recognizing that when we enter into the Mass, we are entering into another world with its own symbols and language. Even when the language of the Mass is the vernacular, it is not the casual vernacular or the street language that we normally use. In some cases, the words are elevated by chant. In any case, the precision and simplicity of the words that are used help us realize we are in a different space, and they require increased attention. Much is said and accomplished in very few words. The language of prayer has its own cadence and grammar. Although the participants speak and sing occasionally, the majority of the Mass is spent listening. The faithful are instructed to participate actively in both speaking and silence, however: "The people, for their part, should associate themselves with the Priest in faith and in silence, as well as by means of their interventions as prescribed in the course of the Eucharistic Prayer" (*GIRM* 147). This requires an interior shift to this new language.

On the one hand, this shift to another language with its ritual gestures, in this different space, can make us feel as if we are entering into an adventurous new world, like C. S. Lewis's Narnia. It may emotionally recall the childhood experience of going to a new house with all its mysterious passageways and artifacts to discover. It may transport us to a place that is somewhat familiar but also very different, like J. R. R. Tolkien's Middle Earth. Sometimes parents rightly tell their small children as they enter a church that it is "God's house." For some children, that phrase spontaneously brings an experience of awe and wonder as they are moved to see everything with new eyes because it is such a special and important house.

In preparing in silence with the intention of seeing things with new eyes and in preparing to enter into a reality with different words, we must purify our words and concepts. In the space of the church, the word *Father* speaks only of a divine Father who is full of mercy, not the limited and sinful fathers we grew up with. The word *awesome* describes mysteries that are beyond imagination, not just the latest baseball win. The word *Lord* refers to a God who has taken on our flesh and died for our salvation, not a powerful person who lords that power over us. In the silence as we prepare for Mass in our pews and as we enter into the Introductory Rites, we undergo a purification of our words: "Yet, since we are part of this world with all its words, how can we make the Word present in words other than through a process of purification of our thoughts, which in addition must be above all a process of purification of our words?"[57] The *Catechism* further clarifies the necessity of a purification of our words and concepts:

> The *purification* of our hearts has to do with paternal or maternal images, stemming from our personal and cultural history, and influencing our relationship with God. God our Father transcends the categories of the created world. To impose our own ideas in this area "upon him" would be to fabricate idols to adore or pull down. To pray to the Father is to enter into his mystery as he is and as the Son has revealed him to us. (CCC 2779)

[57] Pope Benedict XVI, Homily at a Eucharistic Concelebration with Members of the International Theological Commission, October 6, 2006.

Learning ascetical silence

Mary's example

As mentioned in the previous chapter, Mary's interior integration and the particular "shape" of her Immaculate Heart provide a perfect receptacle for the Divine Word. She does not need to purify her heart in the same way we do. All the same, her heart is made of flesh, and she needs to guard and nourish her heart and to nourish her imagination in the same ways we do. Just as her immaculate body needs the same nutrition as ours, so her immaculate imagination, feelings, reason, and will need healthy stimulation and care, just as ours do. Mary's senses need to be nourished with beauty. Her imagination needs to be filled with loving faces, good dreams, and holy images. She needs time for prayer and the structures of religious practice.

Drawing insight from the anthropology of St. Thomas Aquinas, the psychologist Dr. Conrad Baars proposes the kinds of stimulation that nourish the heart:

> [A person] must create opportunities and time for plentiful exposure to the immediate sources of nourishment of his "heart": the beauty of nature, pleasurable activities (fishing, playing, swimming, skiing and many others), the arts, philosophy, the Scriptures, meditation, divine contemplation — in short to all that is good, beautiful and true. Such exposures stimulate his emotions of love, joy and desire. He should avoid stimulation of more than one sense at a time, so he can give his full attention to what he senses via one sense. A good example of this is the avoidance of background music while eating, studying, sunbathing, etc.[58]

---

[58] Baars, *Feeling and Healing Your Emotions*, 167–168.

We can imagine our Lady taking time for beauty, for play, and for Scripture, meditation, and divine contemplation. We can delight in the love, joy, and desire that fill her Immaculate Heart. We can imagine her being single-hearted, focusing on one thing at a time and even one sense at a time, drinking in a beautiful sunset with her eyes or using her ears to enjoy the sound of the birds' songs. Nazareth and Bethlehem are physically beautiful places. The decades that Mary has spent in Nazareth must have nourished her senses, her imagination, and her heart in ways that have kept her fully alive—never spoiling but always nourishing in her humanity the effects of the sanctifying grace she received at conception.

Mary's Immaculate Heart also recoils at evil. Although her interior integration gives her great resilience, her heart is particularly sensitive to ugliness and evil. Exposure to evil does damage to our humanity, and we should always seek distance and refuge from it if we can, as Dr. Baars notes in the continuation of the previous quotation:

> By the same token he should avoid exposure to the bad, the ugly and false, so abundant in our secular, man-centered, utilitarian society that recognizes fewer and fewer absolute moral truths and God, and is bored by natural goodness and beauty.[59]

Mary suffers even more from the evil that she encounters than we suffer from evil. Although she never falls into pride, thinking herself superior to others, she can see the immorality and hear the lies of the sinners around her. Their behavior strikes her heart, and their lies create a horrible dissonance in her mind. Her response is not to condemn but to pray even harder for their deliverance

---

[59] Ibid., 168.

and conversion. We can imagine how the hope for a Savior grew always greater in her heart, even before the angel greeted her: "Hail, full of grace" (Luke 1:28).

All of this was preparation for her regular encounter with God, always tending the space of her heart and creating a place where she could meet Him and abide with Him. It is an ongoing asceticism for her, then, to wait in hope, especially when she does not know exactly what she is waiting for. She has some sense of her special consecration; some sense of her Son's redeeming Passion; some sense of His Resurrection, His glorification, and the coming of the Holy Spirit; yet, in all these things, she does not know the details. Her waiting in silence, powerless to bring about the fulfillment of her hope, is like our waiting for the beginning of Mass, powerless to carry it out on our own. Mary can teach us the ways to prepare our hearts by regularly nourishing them with goodness, beauty, and truth. She can teach us to endure the times of painful waiting, never losing hope in the power of the Lord's Redemption.

Learning from St. Benedict

St. Benedict taught his monks to "diligently cultivate silence at all times" (RB 42:1). He saw silence as having value in itself and reminded his monks that "there are times when good words are to be left unsaid out of esteem for silence" (RB 6:2). Furthermore, quoting Proverbs 10:19, he wrote: "In a flood of words you will not avoid sin" (RB 6:5). Although St. Benedict valued the restraint of speech for the sake of learning from the Master (RB 6:6) or listening to God in prayer (RB 52:2–5), he also promoted the ascetical practice of simply cultivating silence, even offering that as a Lenten discipline, as he encouraged his monks to deny themselves some "needless talking and idle jesting" (RB 49:7).

St. Benedict taught a watchfulness that also helps us to observe our thoughts and feelings and can help us to ground ourselves in God's presence. In his chapter on "Tools for Good Works," he promotes this practice by first encouraging the monk to remember that he is always in God's presence. Although this could be taken in a fearful way, it should rather be understood in a loving way. Our loving God cannot take His eyes off us. With this in mind, we can be watchful of ourselves with gentleness as we are aware that our loving Father is also watching over us: "Hour by hour keep careful watch over all you do, aware that God's gaze is upon you, wherever you may be" (RB 4:48–49).

Furthermore, St. Benedict instructs us that by emptying ourselves of wrongful thoughts, we can cultivate an interior silence that can receive God's Word: "As soon as wrongful thoughts come into your heart, dash them against Christ and disclose them to your spiritual father" (RB 4:50). This calls to mind the simple practice of the Jesus Prayer, which developed especially in the Christian East after St. Benedict's time. In offering the Jesus Prayer, we repeat quietly and lovingly the words "Lord Jesus Christ, Son of God, have mercy on me, a sinner." Steadily repeating this prayer is a way to gently empty our minds of the wrongful thoughts that enter them. An analogous practice from St. Benedict's time is the use of a verse from Psalm 70: "God, come to my assistance. Lord, make haste to help me." Whatever words are used, these are concrete ways to dash our wrongful thoughts against Christ, as St. Benedict teaches.[60]

These practices to cultivate silence build on the practices, mentioned in the last chapter, involving exposing ourselves to

---

[60] Fr. Thomas Acklin and Fr. Boniface Hicks, *Personal Prayer: A Guide for Receiving the Father's Love* (Steubenville, OH: Emmaus Road Publishing, 2020), 231ff.

beauty, truth, and goodness, limiting the amount of stimulation that barrages our senses, and limiting the ugliness that we take in. Furthermore, we should hold back our idle chatter and develop some comfort with just being in silence. In our modern times, we should also add the importance of reducing the amount of technological stimulation we expose ourselves to, silencing notifications, keeping our screens out of sight, and even turning off technology altogether at times. The steady dwindling of the attention span of many people can certainly be curbed by this ascetical silence.[61]

Practicing ascetical silence

As soon as we stop talking, we may become more aware of how loud our interior is. Our mind may be filled with a flood of thoughts, and our heart may be hyperaroused with emotion. As we sit in a safe environment and start to limit our stimulation, this may begin to settle down on its own. When it comes to the settling of our whirling thoughts and emotions or our efforts to stretch our attention gently and steadily, a certain amount will be gained simply with patience. In the cases when our nervous system is hyperaroused, which is not uncommon in our fast-paced society, we might benefit from some techniques. Modern psychology, particularly in the work on trauma therapy, has identified some ways to settle our nervous system through diaphragmatic (deep) breathing and other forms of grounding. Likewise, simply being aware of our thoughts and feelings without trying to judge

---

[61]   The effects of technology, among other things, on our attention span has been extensively studied from a variety of scientific perspectives, as documented in works such as Johann Hari, *Stolen Focus: Why You Can't Pay Attention – and How to Think Deeply Again* (New York: Crown, 2023).

or control them is a starting point for developing greater interior silence and peace.

Long before modern psychology discovered these points, the father of monasticism, St. Anthony, taught them to his monks in the final days of his life in the mid-fourth century:

> Be watchful and do not undo your long practice of asceticism, but be zealous in keeping your resolution as if you were but beginning now. You know how the demons plot against you, you know how fierce they are, yet how feeble in strength. Do not fear them, therefore, but always breathe Christ, and trust in Him.[62]

The invitation to be watchful (similar to what we saw earlier in the Rule of St. Benedict), to cultivate a safe space, to settle one's fear through faith, and to breathe Christ are all wonderful invitations for a Christian practice of grounding one's nervous system as we bring about interior silence and prepare to enter into the Lord's presence. To make it more concrete, Christian psychologist Alison Cook gives the following description of how breathing can settle our hearts and support greater mental health and awareness:

> It may sound cliché, but breathing deeply for even a few minutes is one of the quickest, most effective ways to shift into a healthier mental state; it's a simple way to slow your heart rate, relax tension in your body, and send oxygen to your brain. If you find yourself worrying, panicking, or scrambling mentally, start by taking 4 deep breaths all the

---

[62] St. Athanasius, *Life of St. Anthony*, in *Early Christian Biographies*, ed. Roy Joseph Deferrari, vol. 15 of The Fathers of the Church (Washington, DC: Catholic University of America Press, 1952), 213–214.

way down to your abdomen. Keep going for a few minutes if you can, until you notice the tense parts of your body start to relax.[63]

It is worth noting that silence is not easy. The reflections throughout this book are challenging. We need to be patient with ourselves in putting them into practice. Over time, step by step, we can develop a practice, a habit, of silence. Some works of modern neurobiology and sociology have explored what is involved in developing habits. In his best-selling book *Atomic Habits*,[64] James Clear offers four basic dimensions of habit formation: cue, craving, response, and reward. We need a cue to trigger the craving that leads to the habitual response and produces a particular reward. By making the cue more obvious, the craving more intense, the response easier, and the reward more delightful, we can improve our habit formation. In the case of silence, we do well to notice times when we would like to cultivate greater silence.

What would it take to develop a habit of silence in the sacristy, in the pews, in the car, or in the early morning? One cue in our seminary sacristy is a sign that says simply "Silentium." In one of our monastery hallways, there is a sign quoting from the Rule of St. Benedict: "Monks should diligently cultivate silence at all

---

[63] Alison Cook, "3 Hacks to Feel Better Fast," *The Best of You* (blog), December 5, 2019, https://www.dralisoncook.com/3-hacks-to-feel-better-fast/. In this post, Dr. Cook also refers to the Harvard Medical School blog post on diaphragmatic breathing for further details: "Learning Diaphragmatic Breathing," Harvard Health Publishing, March 10, 2016, https://www.health.harvard.edu/healthbeat/learning-diaphragmatic-breathing.

[64] James Clear, *Atomic Habits: Tiny Changes, Remarkable Results: An Easy and Proven Way to Build Good Habits and Break Bad Ones* (New York: Avery, 2018).

times" (RB 42:1). A cue can also be provided by another person who is keeping silence by keeping his eyes downcast or his hood over his ears.

In addition to cues, we must cultivate a greater craving for silence. This craving will grow as we experience the effects of silence, including its positive effects on our prayerfulness, our inner peace, and even our health. Furthermore, the response—such as stopping our chitchat or minimizing our talk to necessary communications or whispering—must be easy enough not to overwhelm us. The response is easier as the culture of silence is more strongly developed. It is harder to practice silence with strangers than with friends unless everyone present already has the same understanding that silence is the expectation. Lastly, the peace of heart and deeper prayer that silence brings will provide the ultimate reward, but we can also encourage each other and affirm each other when we successfully cultivate quieter environments.

Finally, to bring these points together as a preparation for entering into the sacred liturgy, we should develop the habit of silence as soon as we enter a church. Genuflecting to the Blessed Sacrament in the tabernacle, entering a pew, and kneeling down are further cues to stimulate a craving for interior silence and evoke a response from inside us. As we take several minutes to pray before Mass, we can cultivate a space of readiness in our hearts, already gathering up the areas in which we need the Lord's mercy and calling to mind the intentions we want to bring to Him in the celebration of the sacred mysteries.

As we do this, we can think of the images presented earlier in this chapter. Depending on how we are feeling as we try to enter the silence, we might envision our interior as a snow globe that needs to be held still or a constricted space that needs to be slowly stretched open. We can connect with our inner child to cultivate openness to a new encounter, and we can think of the adventure that awaits us, like entering Narnia or Middle Earth. That way, by the time we reach the Penitential Rite and the Collect, we will have our hearts ready to enter into those liturgical rituals, and we will be ready to encounter Christ as we hear the proclamation of His Word after that.

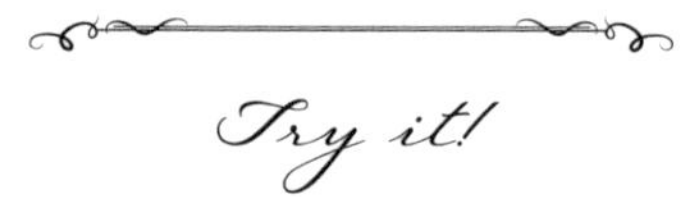

Try it!

When you arrive at Mass, take five minutes to quiet your mind and heart in the ways described in this chapter and imagine making space for Jesus to enter in. After Mass, take note of your experience: Was it hard to settle down? Did the effort help you pay attention to the opening prayer and the readings? Was five minutes enough time to settle your mind and heart? Explain.

For further reflection

✦ St. Augustine had a difficult time entering into silence: he fled from his interior and sought control in external things. How do you identify with his experience? What are some ways you struggle to enter into the silence of the Mass? How do you distract yourself intentionally or unintentionally?

✦ In this chapter there were several images used for making space in our hearts (cleaning out an inner room, stretching open our hearts, settling a snow globe). Which of these are particularly helpful for you? What practices or images do you use when you are trying to settle down and focus on something?

✛ In this chapter there were several images used for making ourselves more vulnerable in prayer (imagining ourselves as a little child, imagining a particular image for God, imagining the Mass as another world, like Narnia or Middle Earth). Which of these are particularly helpful for you? What practices or images do you use when you are trying to become more vulnerable in prayer?

✛ Did you try to practice silence in the way described at the end of the chapter? How did that go? What are some concrete steps you can commit to (cue, craving, response, reward) in order to build a habit of silence?

✛ Which practices help you enter into the Mass better? What keeps you from practicing these regularly?

3

Encountering the Word (Mystical)

At the beginning, we need to put effort into keeping silence;
but if we are faithful to this practice, little by little, out of our
silence something comes to birth within us that attracts us toward
silence more and more strongly. This is why it is not permitted
for each person to speak whenever he wants, about whatever
he wants, to whomsoever he wants, as much as he wants.[65]

Ascetical silence requires stopping the noise and making a space for the Lord. Stopping the noise is not enough, however. Our silent preparation—before Mass and in the Introductory Rites—is for the sake of encounter: "By silence and by singing, the people make this divine word their own" (*GIRM* 55). We are not engaging in the asceticism of silence just for the sake of penance or in hopes of achieving a psychological state of calm but, rather, to make room for an encounter. At the Synod on the Word of God, "a good number of Synod Fathers insisted on the importance of silence in relation to the word of God and its reception in the lives

---

[65] Carthusian Statutes, 14.1–2, quoted in Dom Dysmas de Lassus, *Abuses in the Religious Life and the Path to Healing* (Manchester, NH: Sophia Institute Press, 2023), 54.

of the faithful. The word, in fact, can only be spoken and heard in silence, outward and inward."[66]

Clearly, the Liturgy of the Word is not a time of physical silence (a lack of sound waves), but the silence we are focusing on here is the silence of listening. It is important to reinforce the silence of listening with punctuated moments of external silence, however, as indicated by the *GIRM*:

> The Liturgy of the Word is to be celebrated in such a way as to favor meditation, and so any kind of haste such as hinders recollection is clearly to be avoided. In the course of it, brief periods of silence are also appropriate, accommodated to the assembled congregation; by means of these, under the action of the Holy Spirit, the Word of God may be grasped by the heart and a response through prayer may be prepared. It may be appropriate to observe such periods of silence, for example, before the Liturgy of the Word itself begins, after the First and Second Reading, and lastly at the conclusion of the Homily. (56)

We hold open the interior space, cultivated in the silence of preparation, to listen to the Word and make room for an encounter with God. This is an active silence, an active listening that requires attention and effort. As Pope St. John Paul II expresses it: "Worshippers are not passive, for instance, when listening to the readings or the homily, or following the prayers of the celebrant, and the chants and music of the liturgy. These are experiences of silence and stillness, but they are in their own way profoundly active."[67]

---

[66] Pope Benedict XVI, *Verbum Domini* 66.

[67] Pope St. John Paul II, Address to the Bishops of the Episcopal Conference of the United States of America.

Pope Benedict XVI observes the importance of silence as the environmental condition for listening to God, or, we could say, for having an encounter with God:

> Silence is the environmental condition most conducive to contemplation, to listening to God and to meditation. The very fact of enjoying silence and letting ourselves be "filled", so to speak, with silence, disposes us to prayer. The great prophet Elijah on Mount Horeb—that is, Sinai—experienced a strong squall, then an earthquake and finally flashes of fire, but he did not recognize God's voice in them; instead, he recognized it in a light breeze (cf. 1 Kings 19:11–13).[68]

We are hoping to silence noise so as to hear the voice that speaks very softly. When God is speaking the Ten Commandments, He thunders. This is the truth of natural law that should be found in every human heart. It is the precondition for establishing a just society in which it is most possible for people to encounter Him. But when He is speaking personal words of love to our hearts, He speaks very softly so as not to impinge on our freedom. He longs for our free response, and so He whispers such that only those who really want to hear Him can hear Him. Our preparation, then, is for the sake of hearing that very still voice. Like Elijah, we wait out the thunder, the earthquake, and the storm until we can hear the still, small voice that whispers in our hearts.

There are levels of listening that correspond with increasing trust. The most fruitful listening is also the most trusting and thus also the most vulnerable. When we trust completely, we listen and receive what is given at face value, without skepticism or

---

[68] Pope Benedict XVI, General Audience, August 10, 2011.

criticism.[69] This means that we receive the communication from another and let that person form our heart. To say it another way, we give authority to another person. *Authority* comes from the word *author*. When we give someone authority, we make that person a co-author and give that person the power to help us write our personal story.

Having said that, we can note that, unlike the first movement of silence in preparation, this movement of silence requires elements that are not in our control. We are in a posture of listening in silence, but we require another person to proclaim the Word so that we can receive it in silent listening. This movement still requires our work and our attention to hold the interior silence that we cultivated in the preparation, but now it also depends on another actor, who, with the Lord, leads us to an encounter in the silence of our hearts.

It is worth noting that this silence differs from the later silence of adoration and communion because of the response it elicits from us — namely, a response of self-offering. In this initial encounter, our longing is increased through awe and wonder, and we are moved to a response of self-offering in silence that makes room for the next silence of adoration and communion. Adoration and

---

[69] See Judith E. Glaser, *Conversational Intelligence: How Great Leaders Build Trust and Get Extraordinary Results* (New York: Bibliomation, 2014). Glaser describes three levels of conversation in degrees of increasing trust — transactional, positional, and transformational. The highest level takes place in the most advanced part of the brain, the prefrontal cortex, and has the most transforming effect on each individual — measurable in terms of oxytocin and even epigenetics. According to Glaser, the dynamic of this level of conversation is for one person to share and for the other person to be in a posture of openness that is willing to discover.

communion move to a silence of savoring, resting in the mystery beyond words that has just unfolded in the heart.

In the course of the Mass, the voice of the One who takes the initiative to love us already begins to speak through the architecture, the music, and the prayers, but that voice speaks especially through the Word of God. That Word is solemnly proclaimed in the Liturgy of the Word in a reading or two, a psalm, and the proclamation of the Gospel. The increased focus on encountering God through His Word is a particular feature of the new rite of the Roman Mass:

> For in the readings, as explained by the Homily, God speaks to his people, opening up to them the mystery of redemption and salvation, and offering spiritual nourishment; and Christ himself is present through his word in the midst of the faithful. (*GIRM* 55)

Reinforced by the conciliar teaching in *Dei Verbum*, the Church is convinced of the importance of the Word of God. Pope Francis goes so far as to say that the authenticity of the proclamation depends on an encounter: "A proclamation that does not lead to an encounter with the risen Lord in the celebration is not authentic."[70] There is a real, mystical way that God speaks through His Word, particularly in the liturgy:

> The Church has always venerated the divine Scriptures as she venerated the Body of the Lord, in so far as she never ceases, particularly in the sacred liturgy, to partake of the bread of life and to offer it to the faithful from the one table of the Word of God and the Body of Christ.... They

---

[70]   Pope Francis, *Desiderio Desideravi* 37.

present God's own Word in an unalterable form, and they make the voice of the Holy Spirit sound again and again in the words of the prophets and apostles.... In the sacred books the Father who is in heaven comes lovingly to meet his children, and talks with them.[71]

And correspondingly, the Second Vatican Council's Constitution on the Sacred Liturgy affirms: "He is present in his word since it is he himself who speaks when the holy scriptures are read in the Church."[72] With faith in that revealed truth, we should listen to the Word proclaimed at Mass with the same attention with which we would listen to Christ if we were sitting across from Him in a personal audience. That is the reason we diligently prepare ourselves for Mass, emptying out other distractions so as to hear Him and receive Him who is worthy of all our love.

In this way, we prepare ourselves for the silence of encounter. Although the proclamation of the Word involves sound, we receive the Word in silence, in listening. In this silence of listening, we hold the space for Him to speak to us. As He speaks to us, we experience with awe and wonder the grace of being deemed worthy of such attention. (We will focus more on the importance of awe and wonder in the next section.) At other times, we are not moved to awe, but instead we feel an absence. Our internal silence and our human poverty draw us into the silence of God, who cannot be fully communicated in words. (We will discuss this more deeply later in this chapter.) We are mystified by touching the transcendent. In sensing God's presence or in suffering His felt absence, we are moved to open ourselves even more fully in

---

[71] Second Vatican Council, Dogmatic Constitution on Divine Revelation *Dei Verbum* (November 18, 1965), no. 21.

[72] Second Vatican Council, *Sacrosanctum Concilium* 7.

self-offering and to make more room for Him in our hearts. The silence of encounter moves our hearts to the silence of self-offering.

The *General Instruction on the Lectionary* (*GIL*) teaches us that the best way to foster this meditative receptivity is through a slower pace, including short intervals of silence. In fact, the *GIL* says that this dialogue between God and His people *demands* such intervals:

> The liturgy of the word must be celebrated in a way that fosters meditation; clearly, any sort of haste that hinders reflectiveness must be avoided. The dialogue between God and his people taking place through the Holy Spirit demands short intervals of silence, suited to the assembled congregation, as an opportunity to take the word of God to heart and to prepare a response to it in prayer. (28)

This is a significant departure from the approach to Scripture in the old rite, in which Scripture is treated more like the prayers of the Mass, offered to God as worship. The Scriptures are proclaimed toward the altar, like the prayers in the Mass. There is no separate lectionary or cycle of Scripture; rather, the Scriptures are always tied together with the proper prayers of the Mass. The offering of Scripture to God as worship is a worthy exercise in itself, of course. It is a real honor to have one's own words quoted by others. It is even more of an honor when people gather together to recite what a person has written. The thought of putting a person's words to music is even more honorific. In all these ways, we honor God by reciting and singing His words in Sacred Scripture. We acknowledge the uniqueness of Scripture as having been principally authored by the Holy Spirit, and we recite, sing, proclaim, and even memorize that Word out of reverence for it (see CCC 304). We proclaim it together liturgically out of reverence for its Author and in gratitude for the gift of it.

In the new rite of Mass, we aim to do more than this, however. "Although the sacred liturgy is principally the worship of the divine majesty it likewise contains much instruction for the faithful. For in the liturgy God speaks to his people, and Christ is still proclaiming his Gospel. And the people reply to God both by song and prayer."[73] In addition to offering the Scriptures in worship, we seek to foster an encounter with the living God, who continues to make Himself present in His Word. For this reason, the attention of the faithful to receive His presence is an important part of the liturgical action. Well-placed silences and proper pacing facilitate this transforming experience of grace. In particular, the *GIL* advises: "Proper times for silence during the liturgy of the word are, for example, before this liturgy begins, after the first and the second reading, after the homily" (28). A short pause before proclaiming the Word creates anticipation and helps to stretch the heart, as we have reflected on in the section on the ascetical silence of preparation. Taking time for silence after the proclamation of the readings helps the word to settle, and for a person who is quite noisy internally, it can be a chance to reset each time and listen anew.

The Church places great hope in the fruitfulness that can come from the faithful's encounter with the Word. This new dimension of the celebration of the Mass in the new rite is intended to help the Word continue to spread and grow, as it did in the early Church (see Acts 12:24). Especially when attendance at Mass, including a reverent and prayerful celebration of the Liturgy of the Word, accompanies the reading and study of Sacred Scripture outside of Mass, there can be a new springtime of growth in the spiritual life of the faithful:

[73] Second Vatican Council, *Sacrosanctum Concilium* 33.

So may it come that, by the reading and study of the sacred books "the Word of God may speed on and triumph" (2 Th. 3:1) and the treasure of Revelation entrusted to the Church may more and more fill the hearts of men. Just as from constant attendance at the eucharistic mystery the life of the Church draws increase, so a new impulse of spiritual life may be expected from increased veneration of the Word of God, which "stands forever" (Is. 40:8; cf. 1 Pet. 1:23–25).[74]

In the next section, we consider the experience of awe and wonder that can come from hearing the Word and receiving God in His Word with devotion.

Awe and wonder

As mentioned earlier, Sofia Cavalletti applied the educational approach of Maria Montessori to the catechetical formation of children as young as three years old. Cavalletti also understood the capacity of older people to experience awe and wonder, and thus, her powerful insights on the importance of awe and wonder for the education of children are applicable to adults who still wish to learn and grow. Furthermore, having the humility of little ones is the necessary precondition that Pope Francis offers for opening in wonder: "Since the gift of the mystery celebrated surpasses our capacity to know it, this effort certainly must accompany the permanent formation of everyone, with the humility of little ones, the attitude that opens up into wonder."[75]

Cavalletti understood awe and wonder as a deeper penetration into reality. That is an excellent description of what we are aiming

---

[74] Second Vatican Council, *Dei Verbum* 26.
[75] Pope Francis, *Desiderio Desideravi* 38.

for. In the encounter with Christ in His Word, there is a deeper penetration. Christ penetrates more deeply into our hearts, opening up tender areas with His love, and we penetrate more deeply into His Heart, discovering the hidden treasures of His divine providence. Cavalletti teaches us the attitude we must cultivate in order for this kind of mutual penetration to take place:

> Wonder is a very serious thing that rather than leading us away from reality, can arise only from an attentive observation of reality. Education to wonder is correlative with an education that helps us to go always more deeply into reality. If we skim over things we will never be surprised by them. Wonder is not an emotion of superficial people; it strikes root only in the person whose mind is able to settle and rest in things, in the person who is capable of stopping and looking.[76]

Cavalletti is clear about the importance of being able to stop and look—and we might add listen—as well as to settle and rest in things. This was a part of our silence of preparation, and we see the importance of slowing things down enough to receive, to settle, to rest, to ponder. This slowing down with focused intent can yield marvels:

> It is only through a continued and profound observation of reality that we become conscious of its many aspects, of the secrets and mysteries it contains. Openness to reality and openness to wonder proceed at the same pace. As we gradually enter into what is real, our eyes will come to see it as more and more charged with marvel, and wonder will become a habit of our spirit.[77]

[76] Cavalletti, *The Religious Potential of the Child*, 175.
[77] Ibid.

For example, as we hear the Gospel proclaimed, a single word or phrase might stand out. On one occasion, Jesus' exhortation to His disciples as He sent them out on mission struck me in a particular way: "If any one will not receive you or listen to your words, shake off the dust from your feet as you leave that house or town. Truly, I say to you, it shall be more tolerable on the day of judgment for the land of Sodom and Gomorrah than for that town" (Matt. 10:14–15). I heard Jesus telling me that I was worth receiving, worth listening to. That touched a tender place in my heart that had felt rejected or ignored and neglected. And then I heard Jesus say not only that I was worth listening to but that I was worth fighting for. He would take my side. That touched a place in my heart that felt abandoned and undefended. This is a deeper penetration of reality. Normally speaking, it will not happen unless we slow down to stop and listen.

Dr. Conrad Baars drew similar conclusions and offered similar practices for our psychological health, healing, and growth: "Because one of the first principles of affirming living consists in being present to everything that is, with the full attention of one's entire being, the 'mind' must be more silent than it usually is in our 'rational' and rationalizing society."[78] Dr. Conrad Baars was a psychologist who discovered the great work of St. Thomas Aquinas. The anthropology of St. Thomas describes the interworking of human interiority and in particular the interplay of the emotions. The healthy care and development of the emotions are essential for what Baars describes as "affirming living"—living in a way that can affirm the fullness of reality. To grow into affirming living, Baars notes the importance of silence and slowing things down in a way that can engage the heart more fully.

---

[78]   Baars, *Feeling and Healing Your Emotions*, 166.

To the contrary, we are often stuck in our heads, and this is a particular danger in the liturgy. Dr. Baars explains that living from our heads feels safer than living from our hearts and encountering reality. We end up reducing the wonder of being to utilitarian evaluations:

> Normally, Western man meets every situation and person with an abundance of thoughts, judgments, opinions, comparisons, if not prejudgments and a know-it-all-attitude. This he does for the purpose of being safe and prepared to protect himself from the unknown; to make the best use of certain circumstances; to take advantage of an opportunity; to gain information; to make a good impression on the other person; in short, to advance his utilitarian needs.[79]

When the wonder of being is reduced to the measure of usefulness, liturgy starts to be measured according to the clock. We want to move through things as quickly as possible, not allowing room for anything to strike our hearts. We want to extract the maximum usefulness from the minimum time rather than lingering over what is beautiful and allowing treasures to emerge. We lose the sense of awe and wonder, and we no longer allow the mysteries to encounter us in surprising and personal ways. We can contrast this with the experience of the saints.

In the lives of the saints, there are countless stories of those who heard the Word personally when they listened carefully. A prominent example that led to the foundations of monasticism took place in the life of St. Anthony in the third century:

> It happened that the Gospel was then being read, and he heard the Lord saying to the rich man: "If thou wilt be

---

[79]   Ibid.

perfect, go, sell what thou hast, and give to the poor, and thou shalt have treasure in heaven; and come, follow me." As though God had inspired his thought of the saints and the passage had been read aloud on his account, Anthony left the church at once and gave to the villagers the property he had received from his parents — there were three hundred acres, fertile and very beautiful — so that he and his sister might not be in any way encumbered by it. He sold all their other worldly possessions and collected a large amount of money, which he gave to the poor, keeping a little for his sister's sake.[80]

St. Anthony's encounter with the Word moved him so deeply that he immediately acted, in a radical way, on the grace he received. The silence of encounter moves to the silence of self-offering: St. Anthony encountered the word and then sprang into action. This is not only the experience of the young who have so much to discover and so much life to offer, as Cavalletti expresses it. To the contrary, we have more capacity for discovery as we have more experience and insight. She notes that although their penetration of the reality is different, the young and the old can both share a certain experience of newness as reality continues to open up new horizons before them.

God has made our reality rich with bottomless depths because they open into the eternity of His own heart. He reveals Himself in His creation, leaving His pattern, His fingerprints, His love on everything. He reveals Himself even more richly in His Word, and we never tire of hearing that Word or discovering new depths of texture and meaning in it. We can see this clearly from centuries

---

[80] Athanasius, *Life of St. Anthony*, 135–136.

of reflection on Scripture that continue to yield new discoveries, new connections, new correlations with the human experience, and new movements of grace. As St. Anthony's encounter with the Scripture passage about the rich young man moved him to sell everything and go out into the desert, St. Francis of Assisi's encounter with the same biblical passage moved him to sell everything and become an itinerant beggar evangelist in the cities of the Middle Ages:

> When morning had broken they went into the church of Saint Nicholas, and, after they had prepared with a prayer, Francis, a worshiper of the Trinity, opened the book of the Gospels three times asking God to confirm Bernard's plan with a threefold testimony. At the first opening of the book this text appeared: If you will be perfect, go, sell all that you have, and give to the poor.[81]

Although St. Francis's listening encountered God's Word in the same passage St. Anthony heard, St. Francis (and his companion Bernard) were moved to respond with a very different self-offering. This is the power of the Word to adjust to persons and circumstances and to yield new depths. It is truly a living Word. It is for this reason that we do well to spend a lot of time praying with the Word, reflecting on it, and dwelling in it.

Our penetration of divine revelation through God's Word opens us to a penetration of divine revelation in other parts of reality as well. As Pope Benedict XVI describes, we can hope to find

---

[81] St. Bonaventure, *The Major Legend*, in Regis J. Armstrong, J. A. Wayne Hellmann, and William J. Short, eds., *Francis of Assisi: Early Documents*, vol. 2, *The Founder*, chap. 2 (New York: New City Press, 2008), 544.

God in creation even more fully insofar as we learn to encounter Him in the Word:

> Creation is born of the Logos and indelibly bears the mark of the creative Reason which orders and directs it; with joy-filled certainty the psalms sing: "By the word of the Lord the heavens were made, and all their host by the breath of his mouth" (Ps 33:6); and again, "he spoke, and it came to be; he commanded, and it stood forth" (Ps 33:9). All reality expresses this mystery: "The heavens are telling the glory of God; and the firmament proclaims his handiwork" (Ps 19:1). Thus sacred Scripture itself invites us to acknowledge the Creator by contemplating his creation (cf. Wis 13:5; Rom 1:19–20).[82]

Sofia Cavalletti makes a similar observation about the richness of reality that opens up especially before the religious person. As we understand the intricate and complex interworkings of divine providence and learn to see how God works all things to the good (see Rom. 8:28), our whole life can be caught up into a religious movement of praise.

How can we better cultivate this sense of awe and wonder that can transform our experience of reality in general and the Mass in particular? Again, Cavalletti is instructive for us. She warns against two obstacles that will limit our capacity for awe and wonder. One is that "wonder will be quenched if it does not find a worthy object, if it lingers on limited objects: such objects will inevitably disappoint."[83] In the context of the Mass, we are preserved from

---

[82]   Pope Benedict XVI, *Verbum Domini* 8.
[83]   Ibid., 176.

this danger, since we have the deepest and most profound realities on which to focus and receive into ourselves.

The other obstacle, more pertinent to the subject of silence, regards the pace of the liturgy as it moves through its deep words and ritual gestures. Wonder helps us hold our gaze and penetrate the depths of the symbols presented by the liturgy. As Pope Francis notes, "Wonder is an essential part of the liturgical act.... It is the marvelling of those who experience the power of symbol."[84] We need the time and fixed gaze of wonder to penetrate the depths of the symbols in the liturgy:

> We should not give too many things, we should not offer too many stimuli. We should not alter too often or too rapidly the object of the child's attention. In which case the child would defend himself with an intentional indifference to this kind of wearying, continuous movie. If the child does not have the time to dwell on anything, then everything will come to seem the same to him and he will lose all interest in things.[85]

From this perspective, we can understand even more the prescription from the *GIL* referenced earlier, that uses the strong verbs *must be avoided* and *demands*:

> The Liturgy of the Word must be celebrated in a way that fosters meditation; clearly, any sort of haste that hinders recollection *must be avoided*. The dialogue between God and his people taking place through the Holy Spirit *demands* short intervals of silence, suited to the assembled congregation, as an opportunity to take the word of God

---

84   Pope Francis, *Desiderio Desideravi* 26.
85   Cavalletti, *The Religious Potential of the Child*, 176.

> to heart and to prepare a response to it in prayer. (28, emphasis added)

This also invites reflection on how our liturgies are typically conducted. Do they "foster meditation," incorporate "short intervals of silence," and include opportunities to "take the word of God to heart," as the liturgy requires?

A pure heart sees God

Although the silence of heart that we generally foster in the Liturgy of the Word holds our hearts open for encounter, there is a kind of reset, a renewal of the silence of preparation, that takes place in the proclamation of the Gospel. We see this in the first two of the priest's silent prayers. As explained earlier, the priest's silent prayers give us an indication of the texture of the silence the liturgy provides for us to enter into and can be a guide for the entire congregation on how to pray in that silence.

Pure heart and lips to proclaim the Gospel

The first of the priest's quiet prayers is a reiteration of the silence of preparation, anticipating the proclamation of the Gospel. The priest bows toward the altar and prays, "Cleanse my heart and my lips, almighty God, that I may worthily proclaim your holy Gospel."[86] When a deacon reads the Gospel, a variant of this prayer is offered as a blessing for the deacon, but the rubrics prescribe that in the absence of a deacon, the priest says this prayer quietly while bowing before the altar. The ritual calls for a combination of words, gesture, and location that all carry sacramental significance at this point in the Mass.

---

[86] In Latin, the prayer is "Munda cor meum ac labia mea, omnipotens Deus, ut sanctum Evangelium tuum digne valeam nuntiare."

What is the significance of this point in the Mass? The proclamation of the Holy Gospel is a high point in the Liturgy of the Word, and it takes place last among the readings to indicate its importance. Even though the events from the other readings—for example, the epistles or the Acts of the Apostles—may have occurred later historically, the Gospel always presents Christ's mysteries most directly, and so it comes at the end to show its primacy of place. The famous liturgist and liturgical historian Fr. Josef Jungmann states that there is a "strict rule which holds true in all liturgies, that the last of the readings should consist of a passage from the Gospels," and he explains that this is because "they contain the 'good tidings,' the fulfillment of all the past, and the point from which all future ages radiate."[87] The significance of the proclamation of the Gospel is also set apart by the restriction of who may proclaim it. It is ordinarily proclaimed by the deacon in Western liturgies because he is the highest assisting cleric; in his absence, the priest or bishop proclaims it.[88]

The significance of this proclamation of the saving mysteries contained in the Gospel gives the reason for the quiet preparatory prayer. Such a prayer can be found already in the earliest Roman *Ordo*.[89] The content of the prayer focuses on the worthiness of the one who proclaims the Holy Gospel. This is no wonder, since the minister takes on the very voice of Christ Himself. The Second Vatican Council emphasized that when the Scriptures are proclaimed during Mass, it is Christ Himself who speaks.[90] The

---

[87] Josef Andreas Jungmann, *The Mass of the Roman Rite: Its Origins and Development (Missarum Sollemnia)* (Westminster, MD: Christian Classics, 1986), 1:442.

[88] Ibid., 443.

[89] Ibid., 444.

[90] *Sacrosanctum Concilium* 7.

proclamation of the Gospel has the power to open hearts and bring about repentance and conversion, to cleanse our sins and strengthen our discipleship. It is the great meta-story of salvation history, in which every other personal story finds meaning. It brings us into an encounter with the Lord and Lover of mankind. Seen through a spousal lens, it is also the love story or the love song of the Divine Bridegroom, who woos His Bride and gives her His Word before He gives her His Body.

For all these reasons, the text of this prayer emphasizes the need for worthiness in the minister and asks that his heart be cleansed. There is something very personal about the request for the minister's heart to be cleansed. When the priest says the prayer over the deacon who will proclaim the Gospel, he does not make a judgment on the deacon's heart but only asks that the Lord would be in his heart. But for himself, the priest acknowledges his need for a divine cleansing to produce a pure heart for the sake of a pure proclamation of the saving words God has entrusted to His Church. This is one of the "apologetic prayers" that the priest offers—a theme that will reemerge in this course of reflection on the priest's quiet prayers.

"Out of the abundance of the heart his mouth speaks" (Luke 6:45). The most important thing is for the priest's heart to be cleansed and filled with the Gospel that he proclaims. Then, out of the abundance of his heart the words flow authentically, authoritatively, and effectively through his lips. Even with the cleansing of his heart, this abundance can happen only if his heart is also filled with the Gospel. That raises the question of the priest's preparation for Holy Mass. A priest reads the Gospel differently when he has first prayed with it. The practice of *lectio divina* can greatly enhance the liturgical proclamation and should be considered a necessity for every liturgical reader, but especially for the one who proclaims the most important liturgical Scripture—namely, the Gospel. When he has prayed with the Gospel and understands its twists and turns, its unexpected phrases, exhortations, and ironies, then the priest can proclaim it from the abundance of his heart, owning the words and announcing them as if they were his own.

This prayer is to be made as the priest bows before the altar. The gesture of bowing indicates reverence and humility. The fact that the priest bows before the altar connects the proclamation of the Word with the Eucharistic sacrifice. Other liturgical norms also reinforce that connection, for example by directing that the principal celebrant also ordinarily be the homilist (*GIRM* 66). This prayer, with its accompanying gesture and connection with the altar, reinforces who the priest is, his orientation to the mystery of Christ's sacrifice, and his need for God's grace to carry out this ministry.

If the priest will also be preaching, it would be appropriate for him to add a personal word from the heart to ask for God's grace in giving the homily. Pope Benedict XVI reminded us of an ancient prayer that included this request for help with preaching: "Send your Paraclete Spirit into our hearts and make us understand the Scriptures which he has inspired; and grant that I may interpret them worthily, so that the faithful assembled here may profit thereby."[91] Inspired by the spousal interpretation of the Eucharist as described in Pope St. John Paul II's Theology of the Body, another personal prayer I sometimes add is "that I may worthily proclaim your Gospel and woo your Bride."[92] By the grace of the sacrament of Holy Orders, the priest stands in the position of the Divine Bridegroom, and it is his responsibility to pray, preside,

---

[91] Pope Benedict XVI, *Verbum Domini* 16.

[92] I am grateful to Christopher West for this inspiration.

and speak in such a way that he opens the heart of the Bride to receive her Divine Bridegroom more fully, consciously, and actively in His Word and in His Body.

The Gospel, as the high point of the Liturgy of the Word, is a critically important point in the Mass for the silence of encounter. Whether it opens the hearer up in repentance, as it did for St. Anthony of the Desert; or whether it leads the listener deeper into God's call in his life, as it did for St. Francis; or whether it consoles the listener and encourages him, the proclamation of the Gospel is a peak in the Mass at which the Lord can encounter His people.

The cleansing power of the Word

Following the proclamation of the Holy Gospel, the priest kisses the book of Gospels and quietly prays, "Through the words of the Gospel may our sins be wiped away."[93] Having already prayed that God would cleanse his heart, the minister of the Gospel prays again for a cleansing, but this time, he asks that his sins would be wiped away by the words of the Gospel. How do the words of the Gospel have the power to wipe away sins?

In *Verbum Domini*, Pope Benedict XVI comments on the task of priests to explain the performative character of God's Word:

> It is "the task of priests and deacons, above all when they administer the sacraments, to explain the unity between word and sacrament in the ministry of the Church". The relationship between word and sacramental gesture is the liturgical expression of God's activity in the history of

---

[93] In Latin, the prayer is "Per evangelica dicta, deleantur nostra delicta."

salvation through the performative character of the word itself. In salvation history there is no separation between what God says and what he does. His word appears as alive and active (cf. Heb 4:12), as the Hebrew term *dabar* itself makes clear. In the liturgical action too, we encounter his word which accomplishes what it says. By educating the People of God to discover the performative character of God's word in the liturgy, we will help them to recognize his activity in salvation history and in their individual lives.[94]

Because of his familiarity with the Gospel texts, the priest's heart can become dulled to the power of the Word. This prayer can rouse him to remember the power of the Gospel even to wipe away sins. It was Christ's word that freed the paralytic from his sins (Mark 2:1–12), and it was by His word that He gave the apostles also the power to forgive sins (John 20:19–23).

This prayer is whispered to the Lord even as the priest makes the affectionate gesture of kissing the book of Gospels, which also signifies Christ Himself. This reverential kiss again connects the altar (kissed at the beginning of Mass) with the Word and reminds the priest of the power of these sacramental expressions to bring about purification and sanctification.

Furthermore, he whispers it not only for his own sins but also on behalf of all who are present, that the words would wipe away "our sins." This gesture moves his heart outward to the congregation, to whom he prepares to preach. He unites himself with the faithful at this point. He is in need of hearing the Holy Gospel and having his sins wiped away as much as anyone else. The moral unity with the faithful expressed in this prayer can help the priest to overcome

---

[94]   Pope Benedict XVI, *Verbum Domini* 53.

the temptation to "face off" with the congregation and to preach *at* them. To the contrary, he should realize that he is in need of the Gospel and even his own homily as much as his people are.

Entering the silence of God

In the silence of preparation, we take the risk of settling our internal processes for the sake of listening, so that we might encounter God and hear what He wants to say to us. Silencing our interior makes us vulnerable because our inner processes are part of our self-protection. We think our way out of problems. When there is a threat, our nervous system generally energizes into a state of hyperarousal that propels us into a mode of fight or of flight. To choose to remain in the silence is a great act of trust. Our tendency is to be like the Israelites when they found themselves pursued by Pharaoh and his army:

> When Pharaoh drew near, the people of Israel lifted up their eyes, and behold, the Egyptians were marching after them; and they were in great fear. And the people of Israel cried out to the LORD; and they said to Moses, "Is it because there are no graves in Egypt that you have taken us away to die in the wilderness? What have you done to us, in bringing us out of Egypt? Is not this what we said to you in Egypt, 'Let us alone and let us serve the Egyptians'? For it would have been better for us to serve the Egyptians than to die in the wilderness." (Exod. 14:10–12)

They cried out, they worried, they complained, they wanted to escape back into anything that seemed safer, even an abusive situation. And we can understand this. Our distress is animated by threats, and our defense mechanisms help us survive. If the threat remains, the distress can collapse into a freeze response, in which we shut down. This natural defense response seems to save energy for the sake of preserving more internal resources to use in the event that the threat should pass by. We play dead. This is not the response that God is calling us to, however, when Moses speaks on His behalf to the people. Moses calls them to remain alert but to settle their hearts into a posture of silent, expectant trust:

And Moses said to the people, "Fear not, stand firm, and see the salvation of the LORD, which he will work for you today; for the Egyptians whom you see today, you shall never see again. The LORD will fight for you, and you have only to be still" (Exod. 14:13–14). This is a call to enter into the silence of God. God feels absent, as if He does not see the threat that faces us. He seems inactive, as if He does not care. He seems whimsical and unpredictable, as if He would lead His people out of one danger only to expose them to a greater one. God's silence triggers our fears and exposes our wounds. We find ourselves projecting onto Him numerous images from our worst experiences of authority. Moses' call to his people and to us is easier said than done, but it gives a direction to strive for: "you have only to be still." This is entering into the silence of God. We wait on Him and trust in Him to act on our behalf. We take the risk to believe that everything we experience in terms of His "absence" and "inertness" is not what it seems. We trust that He is present but silent, attentive, and waiting, seeing everything with love and compassion, and actually doing the best thing for us, despite what it feels like for us in the moment.

The silence of preparation stretches our hearts to open a space for God. Sometimes He meets us in that space with His Word and opens us up in awe and wonder in a way that moves us to self-offering. At other times, He wants us to remain in a posture of trust, entering more deeply into His silence. That act of trust and love expands our capacity for Him even more, purifying our hearts and preparing us for a deeper encounter. Pope Benedict helps us understand this experience through an ancient description from St. Augustine:

> Saint Augustine, in a homily on the First Letter of John, describes very beautifully the intimate relationship between prayer and hope. He defines prayer as an exercise of desire. Man was created for greatness—for God himself; he was created to be filled by God. But his heart is too small for the greatness to which it is destined. It must be stretched. "By delaying [his gift], God strengthens our desire; through desire he enlarges our soul and by expanding it he increases its capacity [for receiving him]".[95]

It helps us to view our interior this way, as a container that is meant to hold the greatest and most precious gift—God Himself—but has been shrunken or spoiled (St. Augustine uses the image of a jar made for honey that had been used for vinegar) and needs to be expanded or scraped clean. This reframes the painful experience of silence and waiting in a positive light, as interior preparation for something greater. Although it seems as if God is absent and we can fear that He has forgotten us or abandoned us, in truth He is preparing us for more of Himself.

Pope Benedict XVI reinforces our reason for hope in God's presence even in the most desolate moments. God's silence can bring forth anguish in our hearts, and Pope Benedict does not try to suppress our anguish. To the contrary, by being honest about our anguish and crying it out as needed, we can also steadily learn

---

[95] Pope Benedict XVI, encyclical letter *Spe Salvi* (November 30, 2007), no. 33.

to settle into a place of trust in those painful moments, and we will meet God in His silence:

> "O my God, I cry by day, but you do not answer; and by night, but find no rest. Yet you are holy, enthroned on the praises of Israel" (vv. 3–4). The Psalmist speaks of this "cry" in order to express the full suffering of his prayer to God, seemingly absent: in the moment of anguish his prayer becomes a cry. This also happens in our relationship with the Lord: when we face the most difficult and painful situations, when it seems that God does not hear, we must not be afraid to entrust the whole weight of our overburdened hearts to him, we must not fear to cry out to him in our suffering, we must be convinced that God is close, even if he seems silent.[96]

We also have evidence from Scripture that God might be drawing out our honest cries of anguish to meet us at a deeper level with His mercy. God's mercy embraces human misery, and sometimes in silence He draws out deeper levels of pain so that He might touch those places with His healing love. Consider Jesus' encounter with the Canaanite woman. She ran to Him, crying out, expressing the anguish of a mother's heart for her daughter's suffering, appealing to Jesus' identity as Son of David and Lord. "But he did not answer her a word" (Matt. 15:23). This silence has a way of drawing out all our fears, our projections, our insecurities:

> God's silence as sole reply to impassioned prayer is perhaps the most mysterious and trying aspect of the life of faith. What is the meaning of this silence? Should the distraught

---

[96] Pope Benedict XVI, General Audience, catechesis on prayer, February 8, 2012.

woman have turned to someone else to vent her distress? Should she have addressed Jesus differently? Did she shout too loudly, or not loudly enough? Should she not have realized that the incarnate Word, who came to redeem the world from sin, had concerns too deep and universal in nature to trouble over one mother's private anxiety for her child? Was the Messiah going to waste good world-redeeming time on so localized and inglorious a complaint? And was messianic healing not an exclusively Jewish thing, unfortunately for her, a pagan Canaanite with no rights before the Lord God of Israel?[97]

The experience of God's silence is widely considered a critical point in each person's journey of faith. What is God doing in this silence? Although we do not know the details, we can be sure that it is always creative, always bringing forth something new, deeper, more loving. Sometimes it is drawing out some poison of abandonment from our hearts or pressing into our fears of finitude. But it can become like a womb in us. The womb is a space of profound poverty in a woman, because it cannot fill itself, but at the same time, it is the most amazing space, because it is the one place in which newly conceived human life can grow:

Along with the woman, we can simply listen to the silence, certainly with impatience, yet not without reverence. Silence has an authority all its own, especially when divinely appointed, and we must allow it its rights even when it frustrates our expectations. We must allow it to wash over

[97] Erasmo Leiva-Merikakis, *Fire of Mercy, Heart of the Word: Meditations on the Gospel according to St. Matthew*, vol. 2 (San Francisco: Ignatius Press, 2003), 430–431.

us and enfold us. God's self-manifestation in emptiness can go on indefinitely, until God chooses to create something within it better than emptiness; but we must be convinced that our many words are never better than God's silent emptiness in us. We must not, panic-stricken, begin at once to fill it with our own noise. God's silence in us is one of the choicest works of his grace.[98]

Learning to respond to that silence with self-offering and trust is the hardest part of the spiritual journey and always constitutes the key moment of personal surrender and entrance into communion with the final revelation of Christ—on the Cross. The worst silence we encounter is when we face evil and all the worst forms of human suffering that flow from it. Although the temptation of every generation is to offer explanations for that evil, the reality of human suffering, especially the suffering of the most innocent, always evades every explanation:

> There is no theoretical answer to suffering. To provide a theoretical answer—Job is being punished for secret sins, for example—is an injustice to the sufferer. Suffering is a mystery in the fullest sense of the word. It is a mystery of faith. Human suffering, I propose to you, is totally incomprehensible outside of the light of faith. No worldly theory can adequately apprehend it, do it justice, or do the sufferer justice and, therefore, provide insights as to how to respond to it. It remains the question with which the greatest minds have struggled.[99]

---

[98] Ibid.

[99] Lorenzo Albacete, *Cry of the Heart: On the Meaning of Suffering* (Seattle: Slant Books, 2023), 52, Kindle.

We cannot explain away suffering. It leaves us silent. At the same time, that silence is not an escape from suffering or giving up. Rather, it becomes simply a cry from the heart, the cry of Christ on the Cross. Without Christ, our cry becomes a pathetic whimper and will fade into despair. If we are merely helpless creatures left to our own devices and our hope is only in this life, then, as Paul said, we are the most pitiable of creatures (1 Cor. 15:19). On the other hand, the cry of Christ firmly establishes the identity and dignity of the human person in each person's worst moments of suffering. The silent cry of the Son of Man on the Cross, from the place where He bears all human suffering, reveals that when all answers fall short, when all solutions run out, love still remains.

Although sin seeks to separate the Father from the Son, the Son holds on to us and to the Father and never lets go: "Sin and its consequences intend the separation between the Father and the Son. The cross shows that this separation is impossible, and so it renders sin powerless."[100] The Son suffers everything in order to hold on to our dignity, the transcendent value of our life, the purity of our innocence, the original form of our childlike littleness and dependency. The Son never loses sight of the pure creature God saw in us at the moment of our creation—although deprived of sanctifying grace, still made for that grace and for union with God in eternity. However sin and suffering have marred our appearance, even after Baptism, the Son of Man holds the perfect image in Himself that we were made to be and never lets it slip away from the Father's loving gaze.

In this critical experience, when we face the silence of God, we are challenged to remain present in silent faith. We must not fall back into explanations, remaining in the comfortable space

---

[100] Ibid., 59.

of the power of our reason; nor must we flee from the experience, going back to the comfortable space of our limited powers in this life; nor must we attempt to eliminate the suffering ourselves. Rather, we must remain united with Christ, suffering with Him. In this way, we learn the true meaning of our humanity, which is limited in our creatureliness, and thus capable of suffering, but also transcendent because we can be united with the suffering love of Christ, who remains always beneath the Father's gaze, even in the experience of the Father's silence:

> [Suffering] reveals what the human being is. Through suffering, our own suffering, or our experience of co-suffering with someone else, we touch the very heart of what it means to be a human being. Suffering is revelatory of man.... The human being is incomprehensible without Christ. The human being is a mystery of faith. Only faith can tell us who man is, because personal identity is related to the identity of the eternal Son of God.[101]

It may seem we have wandered a bit from the prayer of the Mass in this reflection, but it touches precisely on the heart of the Mass, which is the sacramental re-presentation of the Cross of Christ. The Mass is the event where all merely human explanations fade away, where the suffering of all humanity in Christ is made present, and thus where all human suffering finds its ultimate meaning. Our decision to enter into the silence of that mystery is defining of our growth in the spiritual life and our union with Christ. As we encounter Christ in that silence, we must learn to make a response of self-offering in silence.

[101] Ibid., 58.

Learning mystical silence

Mary's example

As Pope Francis summarized so concisely about Mary, the Mother of God, "*She speaks little, listens a lot,* and *cherishes in her heart* (cf. Lk 2:19)."[102] Mary is a woman who knows how to listen. Her listening is not just a matter of gathering information but, rather, a listening that allows the Word she hears to form her heart and even to take life in her womb. This is a listening we could describe as "vulnerable listening" or "vulnerable attentiveness."[103]

Vulnerable listening makes the heart like soft wax so that what is heard can make an impression. Vulnerable listening is combined with trust—not listening with a skeptical ear but opening to receive uncritically as truth what is being proclaimed. Such a high degree of trust must be earned slowly in human relationships, but it is the kind of trust that we can have more quickly in the Word of God. It is a matter of listening in faith. As the woman of faith, Mary is one who listens very vulnerably to the Word. Even when she questions the angel, we can understand it as a matter of clarification for the sake of deeper understanding and receptivity.[104]

Furthermore, Mary holds up her own life next to the Word she receives in order to understand the meaning of events more clearly

---

[102] Pope Francis, General Audience, catechesis on discernment 14: Spiritual accompaniment, January 4, 2023.

[103] Fr. Thomas Acklin and Fr. Boniface Hicks, *Spiritual Direction: A Guide for Sharing the Father's Love* (Steubenville, OH: Emmaus Road Publishing, 2017), 78.

[104] Although her question to the angel is often translated "How can this be …?" the Greek would be better translated as "How *will* this be …?" See the footnote for Luke 1:34 in Curtis Mitch and Scott Hahn, eds., *Ignatius Catholic Study Bible: New Testament, Second Catholic Edition* (San Francisco: Ignatius Press, 2010).

in the light of the Word of God. We see this in several ways. One is in the verb used to describe her reflections after certain events: she "ponders" them. In Greek, this is *symballō*, which means "to throw together." She puts things together in her heart as she thinks about what has taken place.

We see this also in Mary's song of praise, the Magnificat, which she sings after she hears Elizabeth's greeting and receives her blessing: "The *Magnificat* is imbued with themes and imagery from the [Old Testament]. It closely resembles the Song of Hannah in 1 Sam 2:1–10, while other passages illumine the background (Ps 89:10, 13; 98:3; 111:9; Sir 33:12; Hab 3:18)."[105] Mary has taken in much of the Scripture that was available to her (the Old Testament) and has learned to see her own life in its light and to understand the movements and themes of her story in light of that great story of salvation.

In these ways, Mary is an example for us, a woman who listens vulnerably and allows the Word to encounter her, to form her heart, to shape her personal narrative, and indeed, to establish the direction of her whole life.

Learning from St. Benedict

St. Benedict begins his Rule with this invitation:

> Listen carefully, my son, to the master's instructions, and attend to them with the ear of your heart. This is advice from a father who loves you; welcome it, and faithfully put it into practice. (RB, prologue 1)

The "master" and "father" referred to here are intentionally ambiguous, pointing both to the abbot Benedict and to our God, whom the abbot should always represent to his monks. The careful

---

[105] Mitch and Hahn, *Ignatius Study Bible*, footnote for Luke 1:46–55.

listening and attention with the ear of the heart are precisely the vulnerable listening that we saw in our Lady and that we have reflected on throughout this chapter. Our listening to the Word of God with an openness to encountering Him happens especially at the level of the heart. It is not just an intellectual engagement with ideas but an openness to being moved by what we hear.

St. Benedict reinforces this word from the prologue by several admonitions throughout the Rule to listen in silence. He encourages regular prayer with the word of God (*lectio divina*), usually four to six hours a day for his monks: "Listen readily to holy reading [*lectio divina*], and devote yourself often to prayer" (RB 4:55–56). Likewise, he admonishes monks to restrain their speech and listen to their teachers: "Speaking and teaching are the master's task; the disciple is to be silent and listen" (RB 6:6). Also, while the reading is being done at the dinner table, St. Benedict requires complete silence for the sake of listening: "Let there be complete silence. No whispering, no speaking—only the reader's voice should be heard there" (RB 38:5). With the intentional connection between the refectory (aka dining room) and the oratory, we can surmise the silence St. Benedict expects for the sake of listening vulnerably during the Liturgy of the Word.

This requires discipline and should not be expected to happen instantly. Rather, as St. Benedict gently counsels in the prologue, "Do not be daunted immediately by fear and run away from the road that leads to salvation. It is bound to be narrow at the outset. But as we progress in this way of life and in faith, we shall run on the path of God's commandments, our hearts overflowing with the inexpressible delight of love" (RB, prologue 48–49). As we make efforts to limit our speech and listen more vulnerably, we can learn from St. Benedict to encounter the Word who is proclaimed in the Liturgy and let that Word form our hearts.

The Hidden Power of Silence in the Mass

Practicing mystical silence

One of the practical steps we can take to become open to an encounter with Christ through His Word is to let down our guard and listen with the intention of being formed, to be attentive with the ear of our hearts. As Pope Benedict XVI exhorts us: "Let us be silent in order to hear the Lord's word and to meditate upon it, so that by the working of the Holy Spirit it may remain in our hearts and speak to us all the days of our lives."[106] This requires us to be aware of our defenses and watchful over our hearts. Is there any resistance to being touched by the Word? Do we believe that He really speaks to us? Are we willing to be loved by Him? Taught by Him? Inspired by Him? Do we believe that He can restore our hope? Heal our sins? Bring us new life and new purpose? What causes us to check out during the readings? Where does our mind wander to? We can practice simply returning our attention to the readings and picking up wherever the reader happens to be at that moment.

Another practice that helps us listen more attentively is *lectio divina*. By praying with the readings before Mass, we prepare our hearts to hear the Word afresh when the readings are proclaimed during Mass. *Lectio divina* is a significant part of the Benedictine heritage and spirituality, but it has been strongly promoted by the popes since the Second Vatican Council. Pope Benedict XVI went so far as to say that "if it is effectively promoted, this practice [*lectio divina*] will bring to the Church—I am convinced of it—a new spiritual springtime." In the same address, he described *lectio divina* as "the diligent reading of Sacred Scripture accompanied by prayer" and indicated that this way of praying "brings about that intimate dialogue in which the person reading hears God who is

---

[106] Pope Benedict XVI, *Verbum Domini* 124.

speaking, and in praying, responds to him with trusting openness of heart (cf. *Dei Verbum*, n. 25)."[107]

Pope Benedict XVI describes the process of *lectio divina* in detail in his apostolic exhortation *Verbum Domini*, and Pope Francis describes it in *The Joy of the Gospel*. There are also many other places to explore *lectio divina* in greater depth.[108] In this context, however, we can simply describe it as a way of reading the Scriptures slowly, even repeating each reading several times, with an expectation of hearing God speaking. One can carry this out most fruitfully in a dedicated space of prayer with minimal distractions and following the kinds of preparation for silence of heart described in the previous two chapters. Furthermore, it will be helpful to read the selections for Mass slowly, while pondering the question: "How do I see God's love for me in this passage?" This question can help focus our attention on the personal way in which God desires to speak to us through His Word.

When a short phrase strikes our hearts, that is a good place to pause and meditate on that phrase, exploring its meaning and speaking to God about it. In the process of reading through even just the Gospel like this, we will begin to understand the Scriptures more and more from the inside, understanding them from the perspective of their own divine logic, and when they are heard at Mass, they will be familiar and comfortable, even if they had

---

[107] Pope Benedict XVI, Address to the Participants in the International Congress Organized to Commemorate the Fortieth Anniversary of the Dogmatic Constitution *Dei Verbum*, September 16, 2005.

[108] See, for example, Michael Casey, *Sacred Reading: The Ancient Art of Lectio Divina* (Liguori, MO: Triumph Books, 1996) or the shorter instruction provided in Acklin and Hicks, *Personal Prayer: A Guide for Receiving the Father's Love.*

seemed a bit strange and foreign at first. By regularly practicing this prayer with the Mass readings before attending Mass, the growing familiarity that we can develop with the Word will greatly assist the potential for encounter during the hearing of the Word at Mass. Persevering in this practice will bear abundant fruit, as Pope Benedict XVI encourages us:

> Listening, meditating, and being silent before the Lord who speaks is an art which is learned by practising it with perseverance. Prayer is of course a gift which nevertheless asks to be accepted; it is a work of God but demands commitment and continuity on our part. Above all continuity and constancy are important.[109]

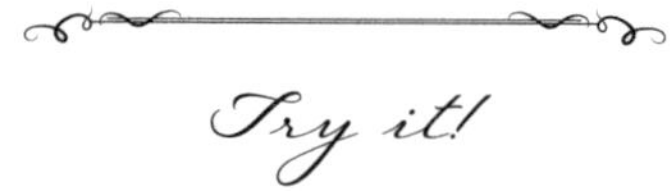

Try it!

Spend fifteen minutes praying with the Gospel reading for an upcoming Mass. Try to use *lectio divina* to deepen your prayer. Then, in your preparation in church before Mass begins, read the Gospel again, try to recall your prayer with that reading, and let that aid your listening during Mass. How does this practice affect your listening? You may have to try this a few times if you have built up habits of distraction during the Gospel.

---

[109] Pope Benedict XVI, General Audience, catechesis on prayer, November 30, 2011.

For further reflection

✝ Hearing Scripture proclaimed was life-changing for St. Anthony and St. Francis. Think of an experience of the Liturgy of the Word in which a particular reading stood out to you in a big way or a small way. How did that affect you?

✝ In this chapter we reflected on how listening can be vulnerable because we allow ourselves to be moved by someone who is speaking to us. Recall a time when you vulnerably listened to someone or when someone vulnerably listened to you. How can you translate your experience of vulnerable listening into listening to God's word in the Mass?

✝ A necessary part of listening well is believing that what we are listening to is important—the greater the importance, the greater the awe and wonder that it elicits in our hearts. How important is Scripture to you? Remember that it is God who speaks to you when the Scripture is proclaimed at Mass. What can you do to cultivate more awe and wonder in your heart, especially for God's Word?

✝ Sometimes we feel as if God is silent, even when we are trying hard to open our hearts and listen to Him. Have you ever experienced the silence of God? What was it like? How did you handle it?

✝ In this chapter, we reflected on how the priest asks silently for the Word of God to cleanse our hearts.

How can your heart and mind be more cleansed by God's Word? How have you seen His Word taking hold in your daily thoughts more and more?

4

The Silence of Offering (Sacrificial)

*Be silent before the Lord G*OD*!*
*For the day of the L*ORD *is at hand;*
*the L*ORD *has prepared a sacrifice*
and consecrated his guests. (Zeph. 1:7)

As we explored in the previous chapter, the silence of encounter can open up into an encounter with God's presence, which elicits from us awe and wonder, or it can leave us in a place of inner silence in which we encounter God's silence. In either case, the proper response to this encounter with God is a silent self-offering. In an encounter with God's presence we return love for love, offering for offering, and give our heart in response to His heart. In the encounter with God's silence, we do not cling to what is our own — our reason, our accomplishments, the safety of our technology for removing pain, or the limits of our philosophies for explaining evil. Rather, we surrender to Him what is ours and remain with Him, letting something greater unfold in the mystery of God's silence than we could ever make happen for ourselves. This self-offering, in God's felt presence or God's felt absence, constitutes a central point in our participation in the Mass.

The Hidden Power of Silence in the Mass

The obvious ritual space of our self-offering is in the Preparation of the Gifts, sometimes called the Offertory of the Mass. It begins, however, even earlier with the Profession of Faith (on Sundays and solemnities) and the Prayer of the Faithful and even in response to the homily. The *GIRM* provides for a period of silence after the homily[110] explaining:

> For in the readings, as explained by the Homily, God speaks to his people, opening up to them the mystery of redemption and salvation, and offering spiritual nourishment; and Christ himself is present through his word in the midst of the faithful. By silence and by singing, the people make this divine word their own, and affirm their adherence to it by means of the Profession of Faith. (55)

[110] In *GIRM* 56, the Church prescribes: "It may be appropriate to observe such periods of silence, for example, before the Liturgy of the Word itself begins, after the First and Second Reading, and lastly at the conclusion of the Homily." In *The Spirit of the Liturgy*, Benedict XVI critiques the period of silence after the homily: "The pause for silence after the homily has not proved to be very satisfactory: it seems artificial, with the congregation just waiting for as long as the celebrant feels inclined to let it go on. What is more, the homily often leaves questions and contradictions in people's minds rather than an invitation to meet the Lord. As a general rule, the homily should conclude with an encouragement to prayer, which would give some content to the brief pause. But even then, it remains just a pause in the liturgy, not something from which a liturgy of silence can develop." All the same, after becoming pope, he incorporated a lengthy period of silence in his own pontifical celebrations. In the Vatican liturgies during the pontificates of Pope Benedict XVI and Pope Francis, there has generally been two to three minutes of silence after the homily.

The Profession of Faith can be considered an initial response of the faithful, which constitutes the Bridal Church, to the Divine Bridegroom's initiation of love in the Liturgy of the Word. In light of this, we can consider the silence after the homily to be both a reflection on all that has been given and a pondering of how to respond. The rising of the Bride, as she stands after this period of silence, could be viewed as a positive response to the proposal of love by her Divine Bridegroom, a radical response of self-offering that she could reach only after serious consideration.

Whether or not the Creed is professed, the standing of the Bride for the Prayer of the Faithful or even her silent prayers while remaining seated, can be seen as her response to the love initiated by Christ in the Liturgy of the Word.[111] After remaining primarily in a receptive posture for the first part of the Mass, preparing herself for encounter and then receiving the mode of encounter initiated personally by Christ toward each individual, she is provided with a series of responses that move into the preparation of the altar with gifts for the Eucharistic sacrifice.

As the priest carries out the ritual actions for the preparation of the altar, his prescribed prayers and gestures, mostly *in secreto*, present a template for the self-offering of the faithful that is meant to take place together with his actions at the altar. Because the priest is the primary agent at this point in the Mass, there is a temptation to think that this is a kind of interlude or intermission between acts, as if the faithful are merely waiting for him to set the stage. Without the proper understanding, music can exacerbate this misconception, seeming like a musical interlude during a scene

---

[111] "The people, for their part, stand and give expression to their prayer either by an invocation said in common after each intention or by praying in silence" (*GIRM* 71b).

change in a play. Rather, this is an important moment of interior prayer determined by the structure of the Mass, as explained by Cardinal Ratzinger:

> In some places, the Preparation of the Gifts is intended as a time for silence. This makes good sense and is fruitful, if we see the Preparation, not as just a pragmatic external action, but as an essentially interior process. We need to see that we ourselves are, or should be, the real gift in the "Word-centered sacrifice" through our sharing in Jesus Christ's act of self-offering to the Father (of which we spoke in the first part). Then this silence is not just a period of waiting, something external. Then something happens inwardly that corresponds to what is going on outwardly—we are disposing ourselves, preparing the way, placing ourselves before the Lord, asking him to make us ready for transformation. Shared silence becomes shared prayer, indeed shared action, a journey out of our everyday life toward the Lord, toward merging our time with his own. Liturgical education ought to regard it as its duty to facilitate this inner process, so that in the common experience of silence the inner process becomes a truly liturgical event and the silence is filled with content.[112]

The faithful learn how to make their self-offering by following in their hearts the example of the priest. Before the priest does anything, there is an eloquent, silent symbol of self-offering in the candles burning near the altar and, outside of Lent, also in the flowers decorating the altar. Then the first optional gesture of the priest is the unveiling of the chalice, which recalls the unveiling

---

[112] Guardini and Ratzinger, *The Spirit of the Liturgy*, 224–225.

of the bride. The silent prayers of the priest include the prayer while mixing the water and the wine, which symbolically mixes our humanity with the divinity of Christ. The second quiet prayer of the priest is the offering that recalls the prayer of the three young men in the fiery furnace. Optionally, the priest offers incense, which symbolizes the offering of our wounds and the cries of our hearts. Lastly, the priest says his third quiet prayer, exposing his sinfulness and asking for God's cleansing mercy.

We can summarize these dynamics of the silent offering in the following way. The candles and flowers teach us to expend our lives in order to give forth our light and beauty. The unveiling of the chalice, symbolizing the removing of the bridal veil, reminds us that it is a self-offering for the sake of fruitful love. The mystery of the water and the wine teaches us that God accepts our limited humanity, and the offering of incense teaches us that He also accepts our wounds. In the prayers of the priest, we learn that we are entering into the white-hot furnace of God's love, and in all of it, we are being cleansed of our sins. We will explore the meaning of these prayers and actions more deeply in the following sections.

In all these ways, we learn to make our self-offering in silence as a response to the love we have already received in the Word of God. In so doing, we prepare ourselves for the even greater love the Word has promised us in love's consummation on the Cross. We anticipate the silent intimacy of adoration and communion that is brought about through the transformation (even transubstantiation) of the very offering we are making.

Candles and Cut Flowers

Candles

Two silent witnesses that are present throughout the Mass but play a particularly poignant role in the Offertory are the candles and, optionally, cut flowers. The *GIRM* prescribes that at least two burning candles be placed on or next to the altar (with an option for more candles, to indicate greater solemnity) (117). Their placement at the altar indicates that their significance is connected especially to the Liturgy of the Eucharist and thus to the sacrifice of Christ. This is easy to understand when we reflect on how they symbolize this very sacrifice. The wax, which, as the Easter Proclamation indicates, is "the work of bees and of your servants' hands," already contains the sacrificial work of creatures, both animal and human. Furthermore, the consumption of the wax provides light and warmth in the fire that steadily burns. In other words, as the bees poured out their lives to make the candles, so the candles steadily pour out their lives to bring forth the light and warmth of fire for the sake of the Mass. In like manner, each participant is invited to offer his or her life to bring light and warmth to the world in union with Christ, who poured out His life to bring the light and warmth of heavenly love to us. In another way, we could say that it is the sacrifice of Christ that strikes the match and brings forth the sacrificial fire that continues to burn from the fuel of our self-offering.

We see the imagery of the candle with particular significance in the Easter candle, especially at the Easter Vigil. There the Easter candle is the one light that burns in the darkness of night. The candle symbolizes Christ, who is the light of the world. We can see that the candle also symbolizes Mary, the one who kept faith even after the light of Christ was hidden from this world through His death on the Cross. And we can see her as the great candle who continued to pour out her life so that Christ's light could continue burning in faith after His burial. The fact that it was the beginning of the Sabbath (Luke 23:54–56) draws our attention to the role that Mary could have played on that most silent Sabbath of Holy Saturday. It was the role of the mother of the house to light the candles on the Sabbath, a role that Mary may have played with the despondent apostles after Christ's body was placed in the tomb. The candles at the altar remind us that as we continue to offer our lives, like Mary, the light of Christ can continue to burn in our lives through the sacrificial silence of offering.

Cut flowers

The *GIRM* provides that flowers decorate the altar as a form of solemnity and a sign of joy (305). For that reason, they are not to be used in Advent or Lent, and their absence is intended to evoke a sense of loss and longing. To evoke such loss and longing in their absence, their presence should be felt sufficiently strongly during the rest of the year. Even in Advent and Lent, they can accompany the festive Gloria, included on feasts and solemnities, and the festive rose-colored vestments, as they can be used on Gaudete Sunday (the third Sunday in Advent) and Laetare Sunday (the fourth Sunday in Lent). The obvious importance of the flowers is in the beauty they bring, especially when they are cut flowers (as opposed to potted flowers), which bring an additional significance in the sacrificial silence of offering. Their connection to the sacrifice is intentional, as they are to be placed near the altar.

In terms of the sacrifice of growing the flowers and the way they can help us to make our own offering, I could not do better than to quote a flower gardener, Carrie Archual. She provided me with some beautiful reflections as I beheld near the altar the very flowers that she had labored over:

> I have pondered how the flowers that I tend to with my heart and my hands and much, much effort, for months and months, are part of the preparation of the altar, a

super-quiet and more hidden preparation—because they are static, part of the ambiance that one doesn't even necessarily notice or pay attention to. And so, well before they ever come close to the altar, the sacrifice has been underway—the sacrifice of my time, in learning and tending, in failing, and in suffering the uncontrollable (weather, weeds, insects, etc.); the sacrifice of my body (farming in the hot months is not a small physical offering); and on and on. And all of this so the flowers can die; so that, when they are at their peak, I can cut them off from their life source and make tangible my sacrifice, literally laying it on the altar. And it's beautiful—I love that it is something of *beauty* that came forth from my hands that is allowed to share the same marble that holds Christ's Body.

Since the first bucket of flowers I brought to the parish, I have found myself quietly wrestling with the thought that these flowers will die, some of them in only a couple of days. I may have tended them *daily* for six months so that they could die on the altar after two days. When I first started handing buckets of flowers to the parish sacristan, I couldn't understand this weird feeling I had, almost of not wanting to hand them over, as though I could put them back on the stems and revive them, but of course, I couldn't; they were already cut, and the offering was in motion. And there was a grief that I would have to do it all over again the next week. Not because I didn't want to—quite the opposite, in fact; harvesting is my favorite part of farming!—but because they were going to die; they were destined for death. And, each day I went to Mass during the week, I would have to stare at them as they shriveled.

Probably 0.1 percent of people in the church would even notice the flowers slowly deteriorating throughout the week. But I notice; I can see the subtle color shifts with each passing day; I know that the petals, if I could touch them, would feel a level dryer—all the things that no one but a flower farmer could notice or would care about. As they slowly, silently, die there, unnoticed on the altar, it makes me think of Isaiah 53:7:

> He was oppressed, and he was afflicted,
> yet he opened not his mouth;
> like a lamb that is led to the slaughter,
> and like a sheep that before its shearers is silent,
> so he opened not his mouth.

The flowers themselves mirror and speak of His offering if we can hear them in their silence; they remain still, silent, and often overlooked—their entire purpose a sacrificial offering.

When thinking of how wounds can become worship with incense [more about this in the section on incense], I also think of my buckets of offerings. It is so fitting that the flowers would die—I think of the way that I wound them, literally cut them off from their life source—just so they can invite us more deeply into true worship. And so they can become their own sacrificial offering of worship. In the field, they fulfill the purpose God created them for, but what beauty it is that they can have an elevated purpose; their beauty is their worship—all they are in their very existence is *for Him*. How much more so on the altar.

It is interesting that I wound the flowers to make my offering; it's like making visible the offering of my own pains.

My own wounds are certainly mingled with my flowers, as are the prayers that I pray while I am tending to them; and I offer them to the Father as a silent act of worship, my own little tangible something to be placed on the altar along with my heart. The priest has the sweet gift of imposing and offering the incense; the flowers feel like my own little bridal offering; and I love that after everyone leaves and it becomes silent and the lights are turned off and the doors locked, the sweet scent of the incense and of my flowers lingers there, continuing to adore silently.

The cut flowers continue to pour out their beauty as they die near the altar. From the moment they are cut, they are already dying. They use the remnant of their life to worship, shine forth in beauty, and direct our attention to the beauty of the Lord's Eucharistic sacrifice. This is a great sign of how we are to enter into the sacrificial silence of the Offertory. We, too, are dying, already a day closer to death than when we first believed (Rom. 13:11). And yet each one of us is also beautiful, a living reflection of the face of Christ. We each have some beauty left to offer, and we can allow our lives to be silently with Christ and point to His beauty, the source of all beauty.

Our humanity becomes divinity

During the Preparation of the Gifts, as the priest (or deacon) pours a small amount of water into the wine, he quietly prays, "By the mystery of this water and wine may we come to share in the divinity of Christ who humbled himself to share in our humanity." This first quiet prayer during this part of the Mass teaches us about the self-offering of our humanity. On the one hand, we know the severe limitations of our humanity. We have already recalled our sinfulness at the beginning of the Mass, and perhaps we have experienced the limitations of our attention span and the embarrassment of our wandering minds or wandering children during the first part of the Mass. It does not take much reflection to note the poverty of our humanity. And some days we feel extremely poor, even more so than usual. This first quiet prayer acknowledges the limitations of our humanity (like water compared with the wine of divinity) and the littleness of our humanity (the water simply disappears into the wine in the chalice and can hardly be noticed). Yet it also acknowledges the dignity of our humanity, which can be mixed into and even be transformed into the divinity of Christ. So this first prayer encourages us to offer our poor, limited humanity courageously and enthusiastically, together with Christ, in the Eucharistic sacrifice.

This prayer was derived from an ancient Christmas oration,[113] and it introduces a profound reflection in the midst of the preparation of the altar for the Eucharistic sacrifice. The Eucharistic sacrifice is tightly bound to the Paschal Mystery of Christ's Passion, death, and Resurrection, but this Offertory prayer maintains the place of the mystery of the Incarnation: He humbled Himself to share in our humanity. And the use of the word *mystery* here also draws attention to that. In Christianity, "mystery" is always fundamentally a wedding of human and divine, of material and spiritual, of time and eternity, of the finite and the infinite: "This is a great mystery, and I mean in reference to Christ and the church" (Eph. 5:32).

It is one of the marks of love that the greater does not destroy or dissolve the lesser but, rather, that it preserves, dignifies, and even raises it up. And so divine love embraces our weak, finite

---

[113] Jungmann, *The Mass of the Roman Rite*, 2:63.

humanity and raises it up, as indicated in this Offertory prayer. Indeed, this prayer is one of the most prominent witnesses in the Western Church to the concept of divinization as put forth by St. Cyprian:

> For because Christ bore us all, in that He also bore our sins, we see that in the water is understood the people, but in the wine is showed the blood of Christ. But when the water is mingled in the cup with wine, the people is made one with Christ, and the assembly of believers is associated and conjoined with Him on whom it believes; which association and conjunction of water and wine is so mingled in the Lord's cup, that that mixture cannot any more be separated.[114]

The meaning of water as our humanity and blood as Christ's divinity was seen differently in other Mass formularies, in which the focus was on the symbolism of the blood and water coming from the side of Christ. This is a natural connection to make. Similarly, there is a natural connection with Scripture found: "This is he who came by water and blood, Jesus Christ, not with the water only but with the water and the blood" (1 John 5:6). While we can still always keep in mind this idea of blood and water—certainly a powerful image in itself—the Church holds before us the great mystery of our transformation. We are truly transformed, by the

---

[114] Cyprian, Epistle 62, no. 13, trans. Robert Ernest Wallis, in *Ante-Nicene Fathers*, eds. Alexander Roberts, James Donaldson, and A. Cleveland Coxe, vol. 5 (Buffalo, NY: Christian Literature Publishing, 1885), revised and edited for New Advent by Kevin Knight, 2009, http://newadvent.org/fathers/050662.htm, quoted in David Vincent Meconi and Carl Olson, *Called to Be the Children of God* (San Francisco: Ignatius Press, 2016), chap. 3, e-book.

Eucharistic sacrifice and the reception of Holy Communion, into God Himself, "partakers of the divine nature" (2 Pet. 1:4).

Another point to consider in reflecting on this prayer for the preparation of the chalice, is that our humanity is not a hindrance to this mighty act of God. Despite the limited, sinful humanity of His ordained minister and the poor humanity of those who have offered the sacrifice of their lives under the forms of bread and wine, God is still fully able to renew His mysteries and, indeed, to bring forth His very presence in transubstantiating the Eucharistic elements. Not only that, but it is precisely *through* this humanity that He comes again into our midst and renews all of His love for us in His Real Presence. As an illustration of this, it has often struck me that by adding a bit more "humanity" in the form of water, there is more Precious Blood available after the Consecration. Of course, the rubrics specify a "little water," and in some places, a small measuring spoon is used for this, but without endangering the proportions, we can still note that a little more water yields a little more Precious Blood. In this way, our humanity is seen to be not a hindrance but, indeed, even a benefit for the Eucharistic offering.

In the 1962 missal, a short introduction precedes this prayer and clearly reiterates the same point: "O God, who, in creating human nature didst wonderfully dignify it, and still more wonderfully restore it ..." God has bestowed a wonderful dignity on our human nature by creating us in His own image and likeness. Then He elevated our human nature by choosing it for the Incarnation of the Divine Son and redeeming it by His love on the Cross, granting it even greater dignity than He gave to the angels (cf. Heb. 2:5). With these thoughts in mind, we can enter into a profound meditation through the priest's simple action of adding water to wine and praying this brief, beautiful prayer as he prepares the chalice at the altar. Concretely, we can think of all the dregs of our humanity at this point in the Mass, including our own weaknesses and limitations as well as those most difficult relationships and qualities of others within and outside of our congregation. We can imagine pouring them all into the chalice while praying from our hearts that Christ would mercifully transform all of these dregs into Himself.

The Fiery Furnace of the Altar

The next silent prayer during the preparation of the altar is an offering of the sacrifice: "With humble spirit and contrite heart may we be accepted by you, O Lord, and may our sacrifice in your sight this day be pleasing to you, Lord God." Here, a commingling of various actions takes place: the priest's self-offering along with the offering of the congregation, both symbolized by the bread and wine, along with the unbloody sacrifice that will take place through the Eucharistic prayer — namely, the re-presentation of Christ's self-sacrificial offering on the Cross. It is especially the magnitude of the ultimate sacrifice that presses the priest to acknowledge his unworthiness and to humble himself and offer his contrite heart.

This prayer is drawn from the prayer of the three young men in the fiery furnace:

> But with contrite heart and humble spirit
> let us be received;
> As though it were burnt offerings of rams and bulls,
> or tens of thousands of fat lambs,
> So let our sacrifice be in your presence today
> and find favor before you;
> for those who trust in you cannot be put to shame.

> And now we follow you with our whole heart,
> we fear you and we seek your face.
> Do not put us to shame,
> but deal with us in your kindness and great
> mercy. (Dan. 3:39–42, NABRE)

It can be a great help if we place ourselves in the context of a fiery furnace as we offer this prayer. It is a prayer of desperation as much as one of great confidence. It is a prayer in which we give *everything* we have, knowing how little that is, and at the same time, with great hope, we "seek [his] face." With this prayer, we promise to follow Him "with our whole heart" while we also know that we cannot do that without His "kindness and great mercy." With these conjunctions of opposites, we perfectly capture what is happening at this moment in the Mass: although we are dying, in great desperation we are offering everything we have, and we know it is practically nothing—only a little bread and a little wine. At the same time, we count on God's mercy, and we beg Him to manifest His presence to us and save us, as we fear Him and seek His face. Furthermore, we are making a promise about how we will conduct ourselves in the future, should He be willing to accept our sacrifice. We will follow Him with our whole heart and walk in the fear of the Lord.

We cannot overlook the connections with Psalm 51[115] either: "My sacrifice, O God, is a contrite spirit; a contrite, humbled heart, O God, you will not scorn" (v. 19, NABRE). This psalm was written by David after his great fall into adultery and murder, and so, in reciting this verse, the priest calls to mind the dregs of sinful humanity and offers up his contrite heart on his own behalf and on behalf of all who need God's mercy.

---

[115] Psalm 50 in the Latin numbering of the psalms.

Although the Offertory prayers of the Novus Ordo have been significantly reduced from the 1962 missal,[116] there is a richness in the retention of this one prayer prayed silently by the priest. As he bows profoundly before the altar and recites this prayer, the priest can place himself and the congregation in the fiery furnace with the three young men and cry to the Lord from his heart. Our need for deliverance and redemption is no less significant now than it was thousands of years ago, but our hope is far greater because we are able to make this Eucharistic offering; and we have absolute confidence that God will come to us and rescue us because He has defeated all our enemies and He "desires all men to be saved and to come to the knowledge of the truth" (1 Tim. 2:4).

Concretely, we can call to mind and even let our hearts be filled with the painful sentiments of all that threatens us in our personal lives as well as at local, national, and international levels. The profound bow that the priest makes also signals to us that he is making this offering and alerts us to make a similar offering and to pray for the salvation of the whole world.

An additional dimension of our prayer at this point in the Mass is the pure miracle that takes place as our humanity is brought into the white-hot furnace of God's divinity. When we think of the power of His divinity, we remember warnings such as God gave to Moses: "You cannot see my face; for man shall not see me and live" (Exod. 33:20). Likewise, the prescriptions about entering into the Holy of Holies in the Temple forbade creative embellishment,

---

[116] The 1962 missal included the Suscipe Sancte Pater (Accept, O Holy Father), the Offerimus (We offer), the Veni Sanctificator (Come, O Sanctifier), and the Suscipe Sancta Trinitas (Accept, Most Holy Trinity).

upon pain of death: "The LORD said to Moses, 'Tell Aaron your brother not to come at all times into the holy place within the veil, before the mercy seat which is upon the ark, lest he die; for I will appear in the cloud upon the mercy seat'" (Lev. 16:2). Further precise instruction is given as well and expected to be carried out, upon pain of death: "Put the incense on the fire before the LORD, that the cloud of the incense may cover the mercy seat which is upon the testimony, lest he die" (Lev. 16:13).

The power and transcendence of God is highlighted in these passages, and we are taught that this cannot be taken lightly. The priest truly enters into a white-hot furnace in the Mass; indeed, "to preside at Eucharist is to be plunged into the furnace of God's love."[117] It is a miracle that he is not destroyed by it.[118] In fact, the reality that he is not destroyed by it reveals that this white-hot fire is, in fact, a fire of love that burns in the Sacred Heart of Jesus. It is a fire that desires to consume sin, suffering, and death and so to purify and receive our self-offering, uniting us to Christ Himself by the power of that same love. As we enter into the fire with acceptable worship, presenting the self-offering of our humanity, with all its limitations and failures, in union with the offering of Christ, we are consumed by God's love, which takes us wholly into Himself: "Therefore let us be grateful for receiving a kingdom that cannot be shaken, and thus let us offer to God acceptable worship, with reverence and awe; for our God is a consuming fire" (Heb. 12:28–29).

---

[117] Pope Francis, *Desiderio Desideravi* 57.

[118] In the Old Testament account, we read about the destructive severity of the furnace when the servants of Nebuchadnezzar were incinerated: "Because the king's order was strict and the furnace very hot, the flame of the fire slew those men who took up Shadrach, Meshach, and Abednego" (Dan. 3:22).

Incense: Wounds Become Worship

Fittingly, the next ritual gesture in this part of the Mass, which is also intended to guide and perfect our own self-offering, is the imposition, blessing, and offering of incense. Although the 1962 missal prescribed some quiet prayers for the priest to offer, the new rite requires that this gesture take place in silence: "The Priest, having put incense into the thurible, blesses it with the Sign of the Cross, without saying anything" (*GIRM* 277). Although there was a beauty in the prayers that the priest offered in the older rite of Mass, there is also an eloquence to the silent gesture of simply marking the incense with the Sign of the Cross. The Cross says everything that needs to be said in that moment.

Incense can be offered at four points in the Mass—at the entrance, at the proclamation of the Gospel, at the Offertory, and at the elevation of the consecrated Host and chalice. We focus here on the incense that is offered as part of the preparation of the altar. This, in particular, is the point in the Mass in which the faithful make their self-offering in silent response to the loving invitation of Christ that has taken place in the first part of the Mass.

What does the incense symbolize? When we consider the incense mentioned in Scripture—namely, frankincense and myrrh—we discover that it is the blood of a tree:[119]

> When a wound on a tree penetrates through the bark and into the sapwood, the tree secretes a resin. Myrrh gum, like frankincense, is such a resin. Myrrh is harvested by repeatedly wounding the trees to bleed the gum, which is waxy and coagulates quickly. After the harvest, the gum

---

[119] I am grateful to Fr. Noel Custodio, a priest of the Archdiocese of Sydney in Australia, for introducing me to this insight.

becomes hard and glossy. The gum is yellowish and may be either clear or opaque. It darkens deeply as it ages, and white streaks emerge.[120]

The incense is the sap, or blood, that comes forth from a wounded tree. It provides an eloquent symbol, therefore, of our own wounds, which were carried by Christ to the Father as He hung on a tree. The incense, in its hardened form, symbolizes our wounds without Christ. We are wounded, and our suffering has no purpose, no destination, no answers, no path of salvation or redemption. It is a hard, useless kernel that sits on a shelf in a closet. In the Mass, however, through the ministry of the priest, the incense finds its true purpose. As the priest imposes the incense on the burning coal in the censer (symbolizing the furnace of God's consuming love), the wounds are transformed into worship. The useless, hardened kernels become a cause for rejoicing. The senses of the faithful are uplifted by the sweet odor of this offering, and, as it has often been remarked by the most innocent children, "It smells like God."

The transformation of our wounds into worship is at the heart of the Mass and is captured in a beautiful ritual symbol in the silent gesture of offering incense. The incense offering also captures a repeated dynamic in the Mass—namely, the collaboration and complementarity between the priestly and lay participation. The lay faithful provide the incense as they present their wounds while the priest is preparing the altar. They do this by calling to mind their sufferings, by remembering their suffering family members

---

[120] Wikipedia, s.v. "Myrrh," last modified July 27, 2023, https:// en.wikipedia.org/wiki/Myrrh. This article references Caspar Neumann and William Lewis, *The Chemical Works of Caspar Neumann, M.D.*, 2nd ed., vol. 3 (London, 1773), 55.

and friends, and by remembering the suffering that is borne by billions of people throughout the world and even by those who are completing their journey of purification after death. They do this by holding out all these hurting hearts to Christ.

For his part, the priest fulfills his liturgical role by carrying out the proper gestures, but it should be more than a liturgical role. He should really know the pain of his people. He should be acquainted with their sufferings, even suffering with them. He should be so deeply in love with his Bridal Church that he exposes his heart and shares in her suffering:

> People thank us because they feel that we have prayed over the realities of their everyday lives, their troubles, their joys, their burdens and their hopes. And when they feel that the fragrance of the Anointed One, of Christ, has come to them through us, they feel encouraged to entrust to us everything they want to bring before the Lord: "Pray for me, Father, because I have this problem", "Bless me, Father", "Pray for me"—these words are the sign that the anointing has flowed down to the edges of the robe, for it has turned into a prayer of supplication, the supplication of the People of God.[121]

There is a moving witness to this movement of spousal vulnerability in the Song of Songs: "You have ravished my heart, my sister, my bride, / you have ravished my heart with a glance of your eyes" (4:9).

The Hebrew verb *livabethini*, translated here as "you have ravished my heart," has been used in literature outside the Bible to

---

[121] Pope Francis, Homily at the Chrism Mass for the Diocese of Rome, March 28, 2013.

describe the stripping of bark from a tree.[122] The bark on a tree is the tree's protection, its defense. Without it, the tender underlayer of the tree is exposed, and a tree with no bark will bleed out and die. The image, then, is of a heart that is so moved by the beloved that it is willing to let down its defenses and expose the tender underlayer that can bleed for her. That blood constitutes its own incense, which can be mingled with her wounds. In this way, the priest, whose heart is ravished with love for his Bride, the Church, brings forth her wounds and his wounds in this act of self-offering worship in the Mass.

As a final point, the tender exposure of a ravished heart and a wounded bride come together in a seal of love. We can explore this by finding the next occurrence of the word *heart* in the Song of Songs:

> Set me as a seal upon your heart,
> as a seal upon your arm;
> for love is strong as death,
> jealousy is cruel as the grave.
> Its flashes are flashes of fire,
> a most vehement flame.
> Many waters cannot quench love,
> neither can floods drown it.
> If a man offered for love
> all the wealth of his house,
> it would be utterly scorned. (8:6–7)

---

[122] Again, I am indebted to Fr. Noel Custodio for this insight, which is also elaborated on in several online articles, such as "Hebrew Word Study—Ravished," *Chaim Bentorah* (blog), May 18, 2019, https://www.chaimbentorah.com/2019/05/hebrew-word -study-ravished/.

Thus, the bride offers to cover, to "seal," her bridegroom's vulnerable heart, which has been ravished, stripped of its defenses. She covers it with her love, her seal. Surprisingly, this covering—the result of sealing the vulnerability of the bridegroom with the vulnerable love of the bride—is the strongest defense: "strong as death." Furthermore, it brings us back to the imagery of fire, "a most vehement flame," that we visualized as the white-hot furnace in the Offertory prayer and that we see again as the burning coal that received the incense in the censer. Finally, we see the immolation of all worldly power ("all the wealth of his house"), which is merely folly ("utterly scorned") in the face of the strength of love. This love is a fire that cannot be put out even by many waters and a treasure that floods cannot wash away.

All of this rich imagery provides a powerful setting in which our self-offering can take place. As he handles the incense, symbolizing the wounds of his people, the holy and loving priest is also deeply moved, exposing his own heart to share in the suffering of his Bride. In one way, he is helpless to alleviate her suffering, as is so often the case when a priest is called to the side of a dying parishioner, a man diagnosed with terminal cancer, a mother holding her dead child, or a teenager in the throws of addiction. On the other hand, it is precisely at this point in the Mass that he does the most important thing for his people: he places their wounds on the burning coal of divine love and transforms their wounds into worship.

The people learn to offer themselves through the hands of the priest, who stands in the Person of Christ the Head (*in persona Christi capitis*) as he celebrates the Mass. They are invited to bring forth silently the wounds they bear, making their hearts vulnerable in this moment and trusting that, as the priest handles the incense, so the Lord tenderly handles the wounds of their hearts. And, as the hardened wounds, perhaps even held back and hidden for decades, are brought forth, they always encounter the fire of love that is strong enough to melt them and transform them. Remembering the tenderhearted suffering of the Bridegroom, whose heart has been ravished, made vulnerable, and laid bare out of His love for the Bride, the one who may be hesitant because of shyness or shame can find needed strength to seal the Bridegroom's tender heart with her own vulnerable love.

Another reinforcement of this imagery of incense can be found in the liturgical rites of the Easter Vigil. When placing five grains of incense in the Paschal candle in the shape of a cross, the priest is instructed to pray: "By his holy and glorious wounds, may Christ the Lord guard us and protect us. Amen." Here again, incense is associated with wounds. In this case, the wounds of Christ receive the incense. With incense symbolizing the wounds of the people, we could say that the wounds of Christ are receptacles into which the wounds of the people can be placed.[123] That means that He has allowed the evils of this world to carve out space in His own flesh in which our wounds can come into communion with Him: "He himself bore our sins in his body on the tree, that we might die to sin and live to righteousness. By his wounds you have been healed" (1 Pet. 2:24).

Although the voice of shame inside us often discourages us from exposing our wounds to Christ, claiming that He will not forgive, that He cannot heal, that He will reject us, or that we are not worthy of His love or of being part of His people, the truth is that He has already carved a place for our wounds in His body. Without our willingness to place our wounds in His wounds, His

---

[123] I am grateful to Fr. John Burns of the Archdiocese of Milwaukee for this insight.

wounds would simply remain empty. His heart remains exposed, waiting, aching until our response of self-offering love provides the seal that is stronger than death. This communion is our union with the power of His Resurrection. And this gives us reason to believe that every wound we bear is a near occasion of communion.[124]

Another aspect of the incense offering in the Mass of Paul VI is that it is accompanied by silence. As mentioned earlier, even when there is music or singing, there are no prayers that accompany the offering, and the incense is blessed without words. One direction we can take for our meditation is the incensation that is described in the book of Revelation, which is accompanied by "silence in heaven" (Rev. 8:1). This silence in Heaven brings us back to the silence of incense offering in the Old Testament Temple. It also invites us to become more aware of the presence of the angels and the saints, whose actions and prayers accompany the silent offering of incense. The silence in Heaven

> recalls the liturgical silence that fell over the Jerusalem Temple when the priests offered incense and the multitudes prayed quietly in the outer courts (Lk 1:8–10). Jewish tradition also speaks of an *angelic* silence in heaven when Israel prays and when the judgments of God are about to fall (Hab 2:20; Zeph 1:7). Here an angel offers the prayers of the saints with incense (Rev 8:3–4) just before curses descend upon the earth (8:7–9:21; 11:15–19).[125]

---

[124] In the Act of Contrition, we speak about avoiding "near occasions of sin." We are often tempted to believe that our wounds and weaknesses are near occasions of sin. It is more Christian, however, to see them as near occasions of communion. I am grateful to Christopher Lafitte for this beautiful insight.

[125] Mitch and Hahn, *Ignatius Catholic Study Bible*, 502.

All of these reflections enhance the way in which we can enter into the silence through self-offering as we unite our whole lives to the Host and the self-offering of Christ that will be sacramentally re-presented in the Eucharistic Prayer.

A Purer Offering

After entering into the fiery furnace with the prayer of the three young men ("With humble spirit and contrite heart …") and optionally wielding the fiery coals in the rite of incensation, the handwashing ritual signifies another intentional step into the Holy of Holies. In this ritual, the priest steps away from the center of the altar and makes one final preparation before returning to the center, summoning the prayers of the people, and entering into the most sacred center of the Mass. The silent prayer that accompanies the handwashing ritual acknowledges the priest's need for grace and spiritual purification as he prepares to undertake this momentous consummation of the liturgy.

The liturgical use of water always draws the mind back to Baptism, the foundational sacrament of regeneration, which is the most important use of water. For this handwashing ritual, the instruction in the missal of Paul VI states: "Then the Priest, standing at the side of the altar, washes his hands, saying quietly: Wash me, O Lord, from my iniquity and cleanse me from my sin." He is then instructed to return to the middle of the altar, to face the people and to invite them to pray.

The practice of handwashing as a preparation for prayer is found even in Christian antiquity, for domestic as well as liturgical use, as witnessed in the *Apostolic Tradition* of Hippolytus and other sources.[126] In fact, some form of washing with water takes

---

[126] See *Apostolic Tradition*, pt. 4, nos. 35, 36.

place several times in the Mass. Ordinarily, the priest starts with handwashing in the sacristy before vesting, as he prays: "Give virtue, O Lord, unto my hands, that every stain may be wiped away: that I may be enabled to serve Thee without defilement of mind or body."[127] The next time he purifies himself with water is when he dips his finger into holy water at the entrance of the church and crosses himself. Optionally, he may then also purify himself along with the faithful in a sprinkling rite. At each of these steps, the priest enters more deeply into the concentric circles of the sacred rites until he arrives at the very center in the Eucharistic Prayer itself. The handwashing at the Offertory is thus one final step of purification before crossing into the heart of the Sacred Mysteries.

Although the ritual has been adjusted slightly in various places for practical reasons, from the outset the primary emphasis was on spiritual purification, as Josef Jungmann observed in his two-volume history of the Roman Rite: "From the very start the symbolic meaning of the act was stressed."[128] Jungmann also provides a helpful explanation for this ritual action: "It is natural that we handle precious things only with hands that are clean. Or to put it more generally, a person approaches a festive or sacred activity only after he has cleansed himself from the grime of the work day and besides has donned festive attire. Thus we find in the liturgy, besides the vesting in liturgical garments, also a washing of hands."[129]

Throughout the history of the Mass, this ritual action was almost always accompanied by prayer.[130] The prayer in ancient

---

127 Vatican, *Compendium on the Eucharist*, appendix 2.
128 Jungmann, *The Mass of the Roman Rite*, 2:76.
129 Ibid.
130 Ibid., 82.

sacramentaries was often from Psalm 26.[131] The particular text referring to handwashing is in verse 6, with verse 7 sometimes appended: "I wash my hands in innocence and take my place around your altar / singing a song of thanksgiving, recounting all your wonders." In the old rite, the rest of Psalm 26 was included as well. Although the rest of the text is not directly related to handwashing, it orients the priest to the praise and thanksgiving he is about to undertake in the Lord's house, along with an appeal to receive mercy and redemption. Interestingly, the verse on handwashing in Psalm 26 does not ask for purification but, rather, insists on the innocence of the one praying as he praises the Lord and asks not to be treated as one of the sinners. Only one line in the psalm, verse 11, beseeches the Lord for mercy and redemption: "Redeem me, and be gracious to me." The sense of the prayer in the old rite, then, is not asking for another purification as much as it is a specifically priestly act. The priest stands here in the house of the Lord *in persona Christi capitis*, asserting his innocence as he makes thanksgiving and asks for mercy on behalf of the people.

In contrast, the prayer provided by the new rite of the Mass focuses explicitly on asking for spiritual washing and cleansing from sin and iniquity for the priest himself. It is much more like a repetition of the handwashing prayer in the sacristy or the sprinkling rite at the beginning of Mass. This prayer invites the priest to acknowledge his sinfulness again and ask for God's cleansing mercy before he enters into the most sacred center of the Mass. Seen another way, since the other three usages of water for purification are all optional, this particular ritual action ensures that the priest will seek spiritual cleansing at least once before praying the Canon of the Mass.

---

[131] Psalm 25 in the Latin numbering of the psalms.

Because this prayer is offered in private, it also invites the priest to have a quiet, intimate moment with the Lord, acknowledging his sins and asking for mercy before his final entrance into the Eucharistic Prayer. This can be a time of real humility and gratitude as the priest prepares to take the last, crucial steps in the most important thing he does. The Roman Rite envisions that the priest takes actual steps in carrying out this final preparation. There is a movement that takes place between the handwashing at the side of the altar and the return to the middle of the altar before facing the people and inviting them to pray. This movement provides an opportunity for a movement of the heart as well. Strengthened by his act of humility and the grace of cleansing he receives from the Lord, the priest can move with a determined heart into the center of the altar. Now he is ready. With a strong heart, he faces the people and confidently summons them to pray with him and for him: "Pray, brethren, that my sacrifice and yours may be acceptable to God, the almighty Father."

As the priest is preparing himself for the offering of the Eucharistic Prayer in this way, it is a model for the people's self-offering as well. Along with the earlier prayer reflections highlighting our humanity in the mystery of water and wine, as well as the wounds we remember in the offering of incense, here we offer ourselves, knowing that we are sinners, but trusting in the mercy of God, who always receives us as a gift.

The Eucharistic Prayer

Following the Offertory, the members of the congregation continue to pray along with the Mass, mostly in silence, offering themselves in union with the sacramental re-presentation of the Offering of Christ:

The people, for their part, should associate themselves with the Priest in faith and in silence, as well as by means of their interventions as prescribed in the course of the Eucharistic Prayer: namely, the responses in the Preface dialogue, the Sanctus (Holy, Holy, Holy), the acclamation after the Consecration, the acclamation Amen after the concluding doxology, as well as other acclamations approved by the Conference of Bishops with the recognitio of the Holy See. (*GIRM* 147)

The words of dialogue that are spoken or sung by the congregation are notable and important. They represent a development in the Mass that took place through the liturgical renewal of the late-nineteenth and early-twentieth centuries. At the same time, they are only a part of the faithful's participation in the Eucharistic Prayer, during most of which they pray without speaking any words. This silent, *internal* participation through listening is intended to be full, conscious, and active:

Furthermore, the meaning of this Prayer is that the whole congregation of the faithful joins with Christ in confessing the great deeds of God and in the offering of Sacrifice. The Eucharistic Prayer requires that everybody listens to it with reverence and in silence. (*GIRM* 78b)

The faithful are not merely waiting for the priest to finish so that they can receive Holy Communion. The faithful are expected to engage actively in union with the offering of Christ in love for us and in love for the Father. The *GIRM* also mentions that the congregation of the faithful "joins with Christ in confessing the great deeds of God." Each of the Eucharistic Prayers recounts the great deeds of God. An extended meditation on each of the Eucharistic

Prayers would be a valuable way to prepare for Mass. Book-length meditations on the Roman Canon (Eucharistic Prayer I) have been composed throughout the centuries and in recent years.[132] The other Eucharistic Prayers, brought into use more recently in the Novus Ordo, also have rich expressions of the great, saving deeds of God and would benefit from extended reflection.

While active meditation on the texts can be beneficial for participation in the Sacred Mysteries, another way to enter into the Eucharistic Prayer is to take the posture that Christ Himself takes in His Passion. The very word *passion* indicates the posture of Christ as He enters into the final days of His life—namely, letting it be done to Him. He takes a passive posture, although it would have to be described as an active passivity, because He remains fully in control, as He told His disciples long before those final moments: "For this reason the Father loves me, because I lay down my life, that I may take it again. No one takes it from me, but I lay it down of my own accord. I have power to lay it down, and I have power to take it again; this charge I have received from my Father" (John 10:17–18). In fact, He indicates that this freely chosen submission is integral to the Father's love for Him. This is a demonstration of divine power—infinite vulnerability. Christ uniquely has the power to make Himself totally vulnerable, to offer Himself completely.

In addition to claiming that power and stating that intention in the Good Shepherd discourse of John 10, Christ also demonstrates His sovereign freedom by anticipating the Passion in the very action of the Last Supper: "This is my body which is given for you." Likewise: "This cup which is poured out for you is the new covenant in my blood" (Luke 22:19, 20). In these ritual gestures,

---

[132] See, for example, Milton T. Walsh, *In Memory of Me: A Meditation on the Roman Canon* (San Francisco: Ignatius Press, 2011).

through which He makes a new covenant and commands the apostles to celebrate the perpetuation of this offering, He freely lays down His life and takes on the posture of the Passion: letting all the evil be done to Him.

In an inspiring analysis of the handing over of Jesus indicated by the Greek verb *paradidomi*, W. H. Vanstone reflects on the fundamental shift that takes place in the Gospels:

> What happens in both Mark and John when Jesus is handed over is not that He passes from success to failure, from gain to loss or from pleasure to pain: it is that He passes from doing to receiving what others do, from working to waiting, from the role of subject to that of object and, in the proper sense of the phrase, from action to passion.[133]

One way for the faithful to enter into the Eucharistic Prayer would be through allowing a similar shift to take place in the posture of their participation—from action to passion. In an analogous way, we can place ourselves on the altar with the bread and wine and let it be done to us. We can take up the posture of the Passion, receiving the evils of the world as we are also transformed into Christ in the Eucharistic Prayer. This invites us to bring forth the wounds that we have suffered as well as the evils that we are currently enduring. We can choose to feel the pain of these hardships, knowing that they are not meaningless but are part of Christ's Passion. As such, they can be offerings of love to the Father, and they can be part of our personal transformation into Christ.

---

[133] W. H. Vanstone, *The Stature of Waiting* (New York: Morehouse Publishing, 2006), 44. I am grateful to Dr. Lucas Briola for the recommendation to consult and include the insights of Vanstone into this book.

Vanstone asserts that waiting does not diminish our dignity, but in waiting, we still share in the dignity of Christ, who also waits in His Passion.[134] Although our inclination is to find our meaning in doing, acting, or creating, it is also divine to wait, to receive, and to suffer. Vanstone observes that we have emphasized man's participation in God's work as a "fellow-worker with God," but we could also discover our participation in God's work as a "fellow receiver with God." After all, God placed Himself in a posture of receptivity through the Incarnation, receiving from His creation and from His creatures. Furthermore, Vanstone notes, it would be accurate to describe man's participation in God's work as being a "fellow sufferer with God" where the word *suffering* is not only about pain and hardship but also retains its meaning of willing passivity—letting something be done.

With this in mind, as the faithful listen to the Eucharistic Prayer and wait, they can unite their waiting with the Passion of Christ as that mystery is being made present. Not only by meditating on the texts of the Eucharistic Prayer, which is a commendable practice, but also by letting it be done, they can fully, consciously, and actively participate in the Mass, even as Christ fully, consciously, and actively participated in His Passion.

Learning sacrificial silence

Mary's example

Mary gives us an example of the sacrificial silence of self-offering in her definitive response to the angel: "Behold, I am the handmaid of the Lord; let it be to me according to your word" (Luke 1:38). In that response, she makes her life totally available to the will of God and the Word of God, who, at that moment, becomes flesh

---

[134] Ibid., 131.

and dwells within her. Her radical surrender to God models the ultimate response to an encounter with the Word and describes the movement that we are invited into in the Preparation of the Gifts in the Mass. Mary makes herself, by her totally free choice, as docile to the Word as the bread and wine in the Mass. We can see her in each of the movements of the Offertory, as described earlier: the bride who is moved by love to unveil her heart, the little human creature who adds all of her humanity to the divinity, the one whose heart is pierced by sin and offers her wounds in worship on the burning coals of divine charity.

Mary also makes her self-offering as she encounters her Son on the Cross. Already anticipated by the prophecy of Simeon as a piercing of the heart, Mary remains steadfast with her Son, sharing in His self-offering to the Father. Her immaculate freedom makes it possible for her to remain with Him, and her defenselessness toward love is like His defenselessness toward the Father. There is nothing withheld; everything is offered. In her case, this means that everything is received. She contributes her Yes, modeling for us how to fulfill the words of St. Paul: "In my flesh I complete what is lacking in Christ's afflictions for the sake of his body, that is, the Church" (Col. 1:24).

At the Cross we also see a reversal of the Original Sin, in which Eve departed from God and from Adam while Adam departed from God and from Eve. At the Cross, when there is every reason to run away, to flee the unimaginable horrors unfolding, the New Adam never departs from our God or from the New Eve, and the New Eve never departs from God or from the New Adam. In this way, the fabric of being, which was ruptured by Original Sin, is put back together through the divine love that Jesus offers and that Mary receives and returns, as everything is given to the Father. And this becomes the cradle of a new humanity—a new family into which a new son was brought forth in a new way by grace through suffering: "Woman, behold, your son!" (John 19:26). In each Mass, we learn to stand beneath the Cross with Mary. With her help, we try to remain a little more faithful, a little more steadfast, and we receive a little more new life like St. John, as sons and daughters of Mary.

Learning from St. Benedict

St. Benedict instructs his monks to respond readily in obedience to their encounter with the Lord as they hear His voice, particularly through the voice of the superior. St. Benedict measures the level of obedience through the immediacy and sincerity of their response. He praises monks who respond without hesitation, who "immediately put aside their own concerns, abandon their own will, and lay down whatever they have in hand, leaving it unfinished.... Almost at the same moment, then, as the master gives the instruction the disciple quickly puts it into practice in the fear of God" (RB 5:7–8, 9). The speed of their response is part of the offering. Additionally, their level of silence, in terms of a lack of murmuring, is a measure of their merit in making the sacrificial offering of their will: "This very obedience, however, will be acceptable to God and agreeable to men only if compliance with what is commanded is not cringing or sluggish or half-hearted, but free from any grumbling or any reaction of unwillingness" (RB 5:14).

St. Benedict makes it clear that this might initially be motivated by "dread of hell" (RB 5:3), but ultimately, "it is love that impels them to pursue everlasting life; therefore they are eager to take the narrow road of which the Lord says: *Narrow is the road that leads to life* (Matt 7:14)" (RB 5:10–11). St. Benedict reiterates this point strongly in the conclusion of his chapter on obedience by emphasizing the importance of interior and exterior silence. Furthermore, this must not be a forced silence through gritted teeth or a white-knuckled obedience, but a trusting, loving willingness to find God's will in obedience to the superior's command:

> Furthermore, the disciples' obedience must be given gladly, for God loves a cheerful giver (2 Cor 9:7). If a disciple obeys grudgingly and grumbles, not only aloud but also in his heart, then, even though he carries out the order, his action will not be accepted with favor by God, who sees that he is grumbling in his heart. He will have no reward for service of this kind; on the contrary, he will incur punishment for grumbling, unless he changes for the better and makes amends. (RB 5:16–19)

Through his teaching, St. Benedict guides us to deeper trust and self-offering out of love for the Lord. Ideally, the Mass becomes a ritual context in which we can offer ourselves with abandon after encountering God's love in the Liturgy of the Word.

Practicing sacrificial silence

The Preparation of the Gifts in the Mass is an important ritual for our participation, but it is one of the hardest moments to enter into, in many cases. After the intense listening in the Liturgy of the Word, it feels like a reprieve for the congregation as the ministers in the sanctuary move into action without need for any particular response from the people in the pews. This can give the feeling of an intermission. That feeling is further reinforced by the jostling that often ensues as a monetary offering is prepared for the basket and as the people page through hymnals to find the Offertory hymn.

Rather than lose this precious opportunity to unite ourselves with the offering that is being prepared on the altar, it would be beneficial to take at least a few moments to pay attention to the ritual that is taking place. The first thing is the unveiling of the chalice, or at least the bringing forth of the chalice, which symbolizes the Bride and can remind us of the love at the center of the Eucharistic sacrifice. The candles and the cut flowers reassure us that even as we die, we have light and beauty to offer to honor the Lord. Furthermore, the mystery of water and wine reminds us of the way God loves the offering of our humanity, little as it may seem. If there is incense, it can be a reminder to include our wounds, not withholding broken bodies and broken hearts but letting them be transformed into worship. And as the priest bows and prays, we can remember the white-hot furnace that is really present, even if not physically seen.

It is unlikely that we will be aware of all these dimensions of the Offertory in our participation in the Mass, but some of these elements can be prepared in advance. What are the ways in which you are dying but can still offer beauty and light? What are the ways you experience the limitations of your humanity? Which of your wounds are causes of real struggle and pain in your life? What would the sanctuary look like if you could really see the burning flames of God's love that are capable of taking up everything and bringing us into union with Him?

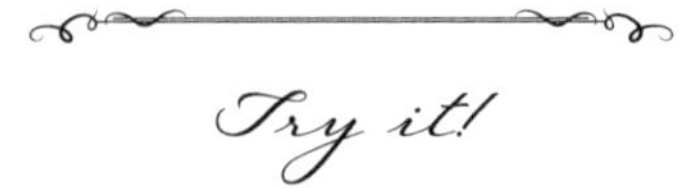

Try it!

The next time you attend Mass, prepare your self-offering in advance. What are the struggles in your life that you want to give to God? Which places in your heart feel fruitless and empty? What wounds—physical, emotional, or spiritual—do you carry? As you think about all these, try to feel them, and then imagine gathering them into your hands like a pile of incense or a pile of bread. Or imagine putting them into a little pitcher like the one from which the water is poured into the wine during Mass. Try to recall this handful of incense or pile of bread or little pitcher of water when you come to the Offertory of the Mass. What is your experience when you try to make this offering?

For further reflection

+ Reflect on the flowers or the candles and their self-sacrificial quality. In what ways are you like a candle that is offering itself to bring light to the world or cut flowers that limit their lives to bring beauty for others to behold?

+ In the Mass, the water poured into wine symbolizes our humanity poured into Christ's divinity. This includes all of our humanity, from the worst parts to the best parts. What parts of you are easy to give to Jesus (e.g., your successes, the parts of you that garner compliments from others)? What parts of you are hard to give to Jesus (e.g., your weaknesses, your failures, the parts that are ridiculed by others)?

+ What are the physical, emotional, or spiritual wounds you bear? What is it like for you to offer them to Jesus—as when the priest places incense on the burning coal of divine love? How are you able to identify with His wounds when you offer your wounds to Him in the Mass? How do you see your wounds on His body and heart?

✝ When the priest bows profoundly and silently prays, "With humble spirit …" he is recalling the prayer of the three young men in the fiery furnace. This points to the miracle that is taking place as the altar also becomes mystically like a fiery furnace. How often are you able to see the Eucharistic offering as a miracle? Reflect on a time when you were particularly amazed at what takes place in the sanctuary as Christ Himself becomes present when the priest says, "This is my Body."

✝ As the priest prays the Eucharistic Prayer, the bread and wine are transformed, and so are all who are letting themselves be transformed. How have you been transformed by the Mass? What are the signs of that transformation in your life?

5

Silence of Adoration and Communion (Contemplative)

Be silent, all flesh, before the LORD; for he has roused himself from his holy dwelling. (Zech. 2:13)

The structure of the liturgy itself provides for other moments of silence. First there is the silence of the Consecration at the elevation of the consecrated species. It is an invitation to direct our eyes toward Christ, to look at him from within, in a gaze that is at once gratitude, adoration, and petition for our own transformation.[135]

Following our preparation, initial encounter, and self-offering, we find ourselves in the Real Presence of God in the Holy Eucharist. We are brought into adoration of and even communion with Jesus Christ. Here we have a silence of awesome power. We are reduced to silence by the presence of greatness. Cardinal Ratzinger expresses it eloquently:

The moment when the Lord comes down and transforms bread and wine to become his Body and Blood cannot fail to stun, to the very core of their being, those who

---

[135] Guardini and Ratzinger, *The Spirit of the Liturgy*, 225.

participate in the Eucharist by faith and prayer. When this happens, we cannot do other than fall to our knees and greet him. The Consecration is the moment of God's great *actio* in the world for us. It draws our eyes and hearts on high. For a moment the world is silent, everything is silent, and in that silence we touch the eternal—for one beat of the heart we step out of time into God's being-with-us.[136]

It is the *mysterium tremendum et fascinans* described by Rudolf Otto.[137] Fr. Robert Spitzer, S.J., summarizes Otto's insights concisely:

After a comprehensive study of historical and contemporary religion, Otto concludes that most human beings have an irreducibly, non-rational experience of the numinous (the interior presence of the transcendent or divine). The "numen" (that which is experienced as transcendent) presents itself fundamentally as "wholly other," having two distinct poles of "feeling-content":

1. *Mysterium tremendum*: a sense of something mysterious, overwhelming, and daunting which elicits from us a sense of diminution, humility, submission, and creatureliness.
2. *Mysterium fascinans*: a sense of something fascinating, desirable, good, caring, and comforting which invites us into its fullness, fulfills us, and

---

[136] Ibid.

[137] Rudolf Otto, *The Idea of the Holy: An Inquiry into the Non-Rational Factor in the Idea of the Divine and Its Relation to the Rational*, trans. John W. Harvey (Self-publ., CreateSpace Independent Publishing Platform, 2017).

in so doing produces a unique kind of spiritual joy (bliss).[138]

This combination of mystery and intimacy captures the irreducible paradox of the Incarnation, and Otto's ideas express the range of experiences that move us to silence at this point in the Mass. This is not a silence we create by our own willpower but, rather, a silence that comes over us, if we let it, as we experience the numinous. It is related to the silence of intimate love when lovers are held in each other's gaze and their hearts are filled with delight. This is the silence that seizes our hearts and perhaps escapes our lips as a gasp as we come to the end of a long climb through a dense forest and arrive at the edge of a cliff, suddenly beholding a vast expanse that stretches out before us for miles upon miles. Although it is not a silence we can create for ourselves, it is the silence that the Lord prepares for us with our cooperation through our first stages of drawing closer to Him. As it was illustrated in some older hand missals, we make our climb up the hill of the Eucharistic Prayer, and then we arrive at a breakthrough peak of presence in the elevation of the consecrated Host and Chalice and even beyond that in Holy Communion.

Otto describes the way we are both diminished and fulfilled. We are humbled in our creatureliness by the greatness of God's majesty, and yet we feel comforted and cared for in the greatness of His Fatherhood. We are terrified by Someone powerful beyond our imaginings and yet also fascinated by Someone who loves us beyond our hopes. There is always an apparent tension between celebrating the majesty of Christ on the one hand and the self-emptying

---

[138] Robert Spitzer, "Rudolf Otto's 'Mysterium Tremendum et Fascinans' of the Numinous Experience," *Magis Center Blog*, May 10, 2023, https://www.magiscenter.com/blog/mysterium-tremendum-et-fascinans-numen.

servant-love of Christ on the other. And yet it is precisely the combination—the fact that it is the majestic King who serves—that makes that mystery even more breathtaking.

The seventeenth-century French bishop Jacques-Bénigne Bossuet describes various movements of love. The first, he says, is admiration. That admiration has a quality of wounding that draws the heart to silence. The heart, wounded by beauty, is unable to find words to express its delight. The delight is greater than any words could adequately capture:

> The first disposition of a heart that wishes to love is a certain admiration ...; it is the first wound that holy love inflicts upon the heart. A dart comes through the glance so that the heart is always occupied with the beauties of Jesus Christ and says with the Bride, without uttering a word: "How beautiful you are, my Beloved, how beautiful and pleasant!" This admiration for the Bridegroom draws the soul to a certain silence that overwhelms all things and is busy with the sole beauties of its beloved; a silence that hushes all things to the extent that it even hushes holy love. It does not allow it to say, I love or I want to love, lest it become intoxicated by talking about itself: so that all that is done by this blessed admiration is to let itself be drawn by the charms of Jesus Christ.[139]

Bossuet offers this alternative description of Otto's *numinous* as being overwhelmed and busied with beauty. This captures the

---

[139] Jacques Bénigne Bossuet, "Lettres de piété," *Lettres* (Paris: Plon, 1927), 250, quoted in Blaise Arminjon, *The Cantata of Love: A Verse-by-Verse Reading of the Song of Songs* (San Francisco: Ignatius Press, 1988), 122–123, Kindle.

double-pole tension of the *tremendum* and the *fascinans*. The meeting of the soul with the Lord in the Eucharist in adoration and communion can truly busy the worshipper with beauty. Countless saints have written about their experience of Eucharistic beauty, describing God's presence, His self-sacrificing love for us, His spousal heroism, and His tender mercies. Although it would be far from true to say that every repetition of the Consecration of the Host and the chalice or every opportunity for the reception of Holy Communion produces this kind of experience, we must observe that it happens and that it is appropriate that it would happen at this point. This is the silence of adoration and communion, the silence of transcendence.

Pope Benedict XVI captures this tension of *tremendum* and *fascinans* in the silence of adoration by an analysis of the Greek and Latin words for *adoration*. The Greek word for *adoration* captures the *tremendum*: "The Greek word is *proskynesis*. It refers to the gesture of submission, the recognition of God as our true measure, supplying the norm that we choose to follow."[140] The Greek word means literally "moving down" and indicates the homage that we have before the great mystery. On the other hand, the Latin word supplies the dimension of *fascinans*: "The Latin word for adoration is *ad-oratio*—mouth to mouth contact, a kiss, an embrace, and hence, ultimately love."[141]

Pope Benedict XVI goes on to explain that adoration becomes union. While revealing the transcendent mystery of His glory and His love for our adoration, God also desires to fill us with that same glory and love in Holy Communion.

---

[140] Pope Benedict XVI, Homily at the Closing Mass of World Youth Day at Marienfeld, Cologne, Germany, August 21, 2005.
[141] Ibid.

In the Eucharist, adoration must become union.... We all eat the one bread, and this means that we ourselves become one. In this way, adoration, as we said earlier, becomes union. God no longer simply stands before us as the One who is totally Other. He is within us, and we are in him. His dynamic enters into us and then seeks to spread outwards to others until it fills the world, so that his love can truly become the dominant measure of the world.[142]

This personal transformation through Holy Communion is a mystery that unfolds in silence. Like the subtle, barely noticeable growth of a small child into an adult, the steady growth of a new convert into a mature Christian takes place little by little in regular moments of silent adoration leading to Holy Communion.

These moments are captured in the Mass through the silence at the elevation of the Host and the Chalice following the Consecration. The priest is instructed by the rubrics in the missal: "He shows the consecrated host to the people, places it again on the paten, and genuflects in adoration." All of that takes place in silence except for an optional ringing of bells at the Elevation.[143] The interruption of the priest's audible recitation or singing of the Eucharistic Prayer for that moment of silent adoration provides a striking opportunity to draw the faithful's attention to the presence of the risen and glorious Lord. As the bells break through the quiet recitation of the Eucharistic Prayer in the old rite, so silence breaks through in the Novus Ordo and draws the attention of the faithful into adoration.

Silence also surrounds the Communion Rite, both in preparation for the priest's reception of Holy Communion and in the

---

[142] Ibid.

[143] "The minister also rings the small bell at each elevation by the Priest, according to local custom" (*GIRM* 150b).

purification of the vessels after Holy Communion. We can learn how to pray fruitfully in these times of silence by considering the quiet prayers of the priest prescribed for those periods, as we will do in the following sections.

Communion with the risen Body
and the whole Church

There are several ritual actions and prayers in the Communion Rite in the Mass. This is a time when the faithful may be tempted to think that their role is only to wait until the priest is ready so that they can finally receive Holy Communion. Especially when there are many ministers of Holy Communion and there is movement to the tabernacle to retrieve the Blessed Sacrament, there can be quite a commotion in and around the sanctuary. This semichaotic preparation for the distribution of Holy Communion can be quite distracting and can appear falsely to be another scene change in the play without a curtain to hide the messy details. Although these preparations should always be choreographed and made as smooth as possible, it is still important for the faithful to focus on their proper task at this time, which is the personal, final interior preparation for becoming a living tabernacle for the Most High God. Here, as earlier, the silent prayers of the priest can be a guide for the faithful in making such a preparation.

In the Communion Rite, the priest offers a silent prayer that is joined with a ritual action. The text of the prayer refers to the meaning of that ritual action. The rubrics indicate that the priest "takes the host, breaks it over the paten, and places a small piece in the chalice." This action has overlapping meanings derived from Syrian influences as well as from its organic development in the Roman Rite. From the Syrian liturgy, it signifies the Resurrection. From its early usage in Rome, it signifies unity. The prayer that accompanies this ritual simply expresses the anticipated reception of Holy Communion along with an implicit longing and the desire for the ultimate fulfillment of Holy Communion in eternal life: "May this mingling of the Body and Blood of our Lord Jesus Christ bring eternal life to us who receive it." We can understand this prayer more deeply when we see its fulfillment in the two other meanings of Resurrection and unity.

The Syrian influence on this ritual points to the Resurrection of Christ as signified by the bringing back together of His Body and Blood. The fracturing of the Host in the Syrian Rite symbolizes Christ's broken body in death, and placing the particle of the Host in the chalice signifies the Resurrection in the reunification of His Body and Blood. This meaning was also embraced in the West, as we can see from the nineteenth-century reflections of Dom Prosper Guéranger: "Its object is to show, that at the moment of Our Lord's Resurrection, His Blood was reunited to his Body; by flowing again in his veins as before."[144] The symbolism of the Resurrection shines a light on the silent prayer and suggests one way that it could be offered. The priest is invited to reflect on the Resurrection as the fount from which this Eucharist flows. It is also a guarantee of victory in the face of all the trials we are undergoing. It reminds us that the Body and Blood of Christ are a pledge of future glory as we long to share in that Resurrection. It gives us a present reason for a future hope in the face of our eventual death. It gives us the strength to have hope in the face of all the ways in which we are currently suffering little deaths at a physical or psychological level. So when the priest prays for the

---

[144] Prosper Guéranger, *Explanation of the Prayers and Ceremonies of Holy Mass*, trans. L. Shepherd (Worcestershire, UK: Stanbrook Abbey, 1885), 61.

mingling to bring eternal life, it can be understood in the light of the Resurrection as signified by the ritual action.

This first meaning is part of the silence of transcendence, a silence of communion with Christ in the power of His Resurrection. Thanks to His Resurrection, we are never alone. His closeness, which always remains in our hearts by grace, is experienced in a tangible way as we receive Him in the Eucharist. This is a *mysterium tremendum et fascinans*. As the priest mingles the Host with the Precious Blood in the chalice, the faithful can anticipate that profound encounter they are about to have in Holy Communion. It is an encounter of love that brings hope; that overcomes death and brings eternal life; that builds on and exceeds every other love on this earth; that makes possible a deeper encounter of love in Christ with every person who has lived, before or since. This last point comes out in another interpretation of this ritual action and silent prayer.

Another origin for the mingling of a particle of the Host with the Precious Blood was in the spirit of unity. In the early Church, a particle from the bishop's Mass called a *fermentum* was brought to the parish church and mingled in the priest's chalice as a sign of the unity of the priest's Mass with the bishop's.[145] With this unity in mind, the priest's prayer during the ritual action of commingling can take on other dimensions. Although this practice disappeared centuries ago, there was a time that the particle from the bishop connected the Mass with the whole diocesan Church, and the prayer served an intercessory role for all those in the diocese who received from the bishop's Host. The current commingling reminds us of that unity and also that salvation is not a solitary affair, but like Communion, it is something that we receive together and that brings us into unity even as it also has

---

[145] Jungmann, *The Mass of the Roman Rite*, 2:312.

a dramatically personal dimension. Seen under the sign of unity, it symbolically expresses that receiving the Eucharist is certainly entering into communion with Christ, but it is also deepening our communion with His Bride, the Church.

Such communion with others brings us more fully into the image and likeness of God, as taught by Pope St. John Paul II in his catecheses on the Theology of the Body: "Man becomes an image of God not so much in the moment of solitude as in the moment of communion."[146] Thus, by receiving Holy Communion, one is transformed into Christ, both by becoming more and more that which he or she eats as well as by entering into Communion with all those who are in communion with the Church.

We conclude our thoughts on this silent prayer of the priest with an eloquent and challenging reflection on unity by St. Ignatius of Antioch. We can consider that St. Ignatius's challenge to unity is imaged in the priest's ritual act of commingling, and that ecclesial unity can be one intention of the silent prayer he offers as he places the particle of the Host in the chalice:

> Thus it is proper for you to act together in harmony with the mind of the bishop, as you are in fact doing. For your presbytery, which is worthy of its name and worthy of God, is attuned to the bishop as strings to a lyre. Therefore in your unanimity and harmonious love Jesus Christ is sung. You must join this chorus, every one of you, so that by being harmonious in unanimity and taking your pitch from God you may sing in unison with one voice through Jesus Christ to the Father, in order that he may both hear you and, on the basis

---

146 Theology of the Body catechesis 9:3 in Pope St. John Paul II, *Man and Woman He Created Them: A Theology of the Body*, trans. Michael Waldstein (Boston: Pauline Books and Media, 2006).

of what you do well, acknowledge that you are members of his Son. It is, therefore, advantageous for you to be in perfect unity, in order that you may always have a share in God.[147]

His Body and Blood set us free

As the priest prepares to receive Holy Communion, he is instructed to pray one of two prayers (nothing prohibits him from praying both, of course!):

Lord Jesus Christ, Son of the living God, who, by the will of the Father and the work of the Holy Spirit, through your Death gave life to the world, free me by this, your most holy Body and Blood, from all my sins and from every evil; keep me always faithful to your commandments, and never let me be parted from you.[148]

May the receiving of your Body and Blood, Lord Jesus Christ, not bring me to judgment and condemnation, but through your loving mercy be for me protection in mind and body and a healing remedy.[149]

---

[147] Letter to the Ephesians, no. 4, in Michael William Holmes, *The Apostolic Fathers: Greek Texts and English Translations*, updated ed. (Grand Rapids, MI: Baker Books, 1999), 139.

[148] In Latin, the prayer is "Domine Jesu Christe, Fili Dei vivi, qui ex voluntate Patris, cooperante Spiritu Sancto, per mortem tuam mundum vivificasti: libera me per hoc sacrosanctum Corpus et Sanguinem tuum ab omnibus iniquitatibus meis et universis malis: et fac me tuis semper inhaerere mandatis et a te numquam separari permittas."

[149] In Latin, the prayer is "Perceptio Córporis et Sanguinis tui, Domine Jesu Christe, non mihi proveniat in iudícium et condemnationem: sed pro tua pietate prosit mihi ad tutamentum mentis et corporis, et ad medelam percipiendam."

According to Dom Guéranger, these prayers are "not very ancient; nevertheless, they are at least a thousand years old."[150] Thus, they were prayed daily by all of our favorite priest saints (as far back as St. Peter Damian, St. Bernard, and St. Dominic and certainly including later saints, such as Pope Pius V, John of the Cross, and Alphonsus Liguori). It is marvelous to reflect on the formative power of prayers whispered quietly by every priest every day for the last thousand years.

The *GIRM* makes a significant point in saying that the faithful would do well to learn from the priest and to offer one of these prayers or a similar prayer at the same time as the priest before Holy Communion. The priest should therefore be conscientious about offering a good example to the faithful in this act of preparation, for the sake of a more fruitful reception of Holy Communion.

The content of both prayers is quite deep and invites repeated and lengthy reflection. Meditating on these prayers helps us to enter into this moment of silent transcendence in communion more fruitfully. Let us begin with the first:

> Lord Jesus Christ, Son of the living God, who, by the will of the Father and the work of the Holy Spirit, through your Death gave life to the world, free me by this, your most holy Body and Blood, from all my sins and from every evil; keep me always faithful to your commandments, and never let me be parted from you.

This prayer's introductory descriptions of who God is and what He has done are very theologically rich and impressive, but it is even more moving to see that richness building toward the central verb, which is the cry of a prisoner: "Free me." The priest

---

[150] Guéranger, *Prayers and Ceremonies of Holy Mass*, 63.

cries out from his bondage for what he knows to be impossible for any power on this earth: for the chains of sin to be broken. Why does he even ask for this? Because he knows he can ask through the power of the very miracle that lies before his eyes as he bends toward the altar and gazes upon the Body and Blood of Christ: "Free me by this, your most holy Body and Blood …"

Then the prayer describes the great chains that are personal to the priest himself. Every priest is drawn from among sinners (Heb. 5:1–4). The priest is helped to remember his sinfulness throughout the Mass, but in a particular way, he remembers it here, immediately before he receives Holy Communion, and so he prays to be freed from "all my sins." The priest knows the way that sin brings bondage and weighs him down by turning him away from his God and his flock only to focus on himself. Even when sins have been absolved, the weight of sin, its lingering dullness of heart, the disordered *habitus* of vice, and the tendency toward self-absorption still cause the priest innumerable obstacles in his prayer, his ministry, and his growth in holiness. "Free me … from all my sins!" The cry at the heart of this prayer is so beautifully childlike in its simplicity and its intensity.

The priest also acknowledges that there are forces outside of him that assault him, oppress him, and even bind him, and so he begs God: "Free me from every evil!" This evil comes at him from the devil working through the world and through the flesh. There is real evil in the world, and some men actively cooperate with it. There are worldwide plots of evil intent that have caught up nations within their destructive force. The priest who hears confessions and who walks with the little and great actors on the world stage knows how much suffering is caused by evil and how easily even the greatest men can be led astray. The priest knows the wicked power of Satan and his determination to destroy all the creatures made in God's image. The man who knows the principalities and dark powers with which he battles in this fallen world rightly intercedes with the one who has conquered the world: "Free me by your most holy Body and Blood … from every evil!"

At its heart, evil is always seeking to undo communion, to destroy love, and to separate us from God and from one another. Whereas the Holy Spirit brings about communion and love, the evil spirits bring about division and isolation. Whereas there is an inherently relational aspect to angels (whose very name means "messenger," and thus they connect at least two parties with a message), there is an antirelational element to fallen angels or devils (the word for "devil" in Greek, *diábolos*, means "to throw apart"). Holy Communion can help to heal the places of division in our hearts as we allow the Lord to enter into the wounds of betrayal, abandonment, rejection, and isolation. In Holy Communion, Christ is the Good Shepherd who goes in search of the lost sheep (see Luke 15:3–7), or like the woman searching for the lost coin, who sweeps our interior house with the lamp of truth until He finds what has been lost in us (Luke 15:8–9). All of this overcomes the influence of the evil one and restores interior communion and exterior communion, with God and with others.

In addition to being free, the priest also wants to be holy, aligned with God's will in such a deep and intimate way that it lives inside him. He does not aim to live the commandments by way of imitation or merely external observance, but he wants them to be part of him, the way his heart beats or his lungs take in air. He wants the commands of God always to "inhere" in him. Here he prays, "Keep me always faithful,"[151] but the Latin verb *inhaerere* is deeper. Its translations include "cling," "adhere," "haunt," or

---

[151] Fac me tuis semper inhaerere mandatis.

"dwell in." The priest wants the commandments of God always to be so deeply in him and a part of all he does that they dwell in him.

The word *mandatis* also calls to mind the *mandatum novum*, or "new commandment," from Holy Thursday. The new commandment sums up and exceeds all the others, and it is the one that cannot be fulfilled unless Jesus Himself inheres in us: "Love one another as I love you" (see John 13:34). As the priest prepares to receive Jesus in Holy Communion, he asks for the greatest effect of Holy Communion—namely, to love as Jesus loves or, more accurately, to love with Jesus' own love or even to let Jesus into him that Jesus may love from within him.

The last part of the prayer extends the petition in duration as the priest prepares to receive the Son of God into Himself in Holy Communion. He asks God for the grace that will never end: "Let me never be separated from you." It is the grace of constant presence, to the point of final perseverance. It evokes a sentiment similar to that of the post-Communion prayer of Padre Pio, in which he humbly begs: "Stay with me, Lord, for it is necessary to have You present so that I do not forget You. You know how easily I abandon You." It is a prayer for the Lord to stay with us so that we will stay with Him.

We now come back to the beginning of this beautiful prayer to acknowledge the rich Trinitarian theology that is expressed in the first phrases. The will of the Father, the cooperation of the Holy Spirit, and the death of the living God in Jesus Christ vivify the whole world. The priest offers this prayer at the altar, before the consecrated Host and the Blood-filled chalice, in the midst of the white-hot furnace of divine love that radiates out to make the world pulsate with life and glow with love. Without the Trinitarian cooperation that led to the death of Christ, everything would be merely fading away, but with divine life poured out from the

Cross into this dying world through baptized souls and Eucharistic renewal, the world radiates again with the power of redemption. The hope of a new heaven and a new earth enters into the darkness of this world and the shadow of death. It is precisely this living and life-giving power of Christ's Body and Blood that we need to free us, to inhere in us, and never to be separated from us.

Finding refuge in Christ's Body and Blood

Let us turn to the second option for this prayer before receiving Communion:

> May the receiving of your Body and Blood, Lord Jesus Christ, not bring me to judgment and condemnation, but through your loving mercy be for me protection in mind and body and a healing remedy.

This prayer of preparation masterfully expresses reverence for God together with trust in His tenderness and mercy. The prayer not to face judgment and condemnation on account of this reception of Christ's Body and Blood expresses a real concern. We are about to welcome the living God into our own bodies and souls. This is no small act. We recall the memorable and terrifying incident of the Old Testament when God struck Uzzah dead for touching the Ark of the Covenant (2 Sam. 6:1–7). And there is something greater than the Ark here. We cannot underestimate the significance of this moment, even after having received Communion thousands of times. This prayer reminds us, first of all, of how profound this moment is and incites in us a little humility and trembling before this *mysterium tremendum.*

This is also a *mysterium fascinans.* We encounter in Christ not only the just Judge, but also the merciful Savior, and so we have confidence to call on His loving mercy. Specifically, we ask that through His loving mercy, He would be for us protection and healing. The phrase translated "be for us" comes from the Latin *prosit*, asking that this reception of Holy Communion would profit us or be fruitful in us. It reminds us of the traditional prayer after the procession out of Mass and the return to the sacristy. In an act of cultural piety, the priest bows his head to the crucifix and prays, "*Prosit*," followed by the response of the other ministers: "*Omnibus et singulis*" (May it be fruitful for all and for each). This prayer for the Eucharist to be fruitful for each and for all is made privately and personally by the priest here before receiving Communion.

The prayer further specifies in what ways Communion should be fruitful—namely, for healing and protection. The priest should never celebrate the sacraments if he is not in a state of grace. Even in a state of grace, however, he remains in need of healing. The journey of healing is lifelong, and the daily prayer for healing offered just before reception of the Eucharist assists him in taking the next step. We are all wounded healers. We each need our own healing even as we serve the Lord in mediating His healing love to others. The Lord's loving mercy will touch and heal every spot in our minds and hearts if we let it.

One place where many of us need healing is in our hope. That hope often lives in a childlike part of us that easily gets buried beneath cynicism and discouragement. Our initial dreams for priestly ministry and our original wonder at the miracle of the sacraments can gradually become tired and jaded. But God wants to renew our first love (see Rev. 2:4), and this can be part of the healing that we pray for as we receive the Lord's Body and Blood, remembering His promise to us: "Behold, I make all things new" (Rev. 21:5). We do well to remember how, in the Exsultet, sung at the Easter Vigil, we proclaim the power of Easter that is renewed in every Mass: "The sanctifying power of this night dispels wickedness, washes faults away, restores innocence to the fallen, and joy to mourners, drives out hatred, fosters concord, and brings down the mighty." The Paschal Mysteries can even restore our lost innocence and return joy to our hearts if we allow them to.

Lastly, we pray not only to gain further healing but to protect that which we have already received. We ask that our receiving of the Body and Blood of Christ would be a protection (*tutamentum*) of mind and body. *Tutamentum* could also be translated as "refuge." The word *refuge* provides a clearer image for us to reflect on. Christ's heart, present to us in His Body and Blood, is our hiding place, where He keeps our bodies and minds safe from the enemy. As we recognized in the other preparation prayer, the priest must be aware that there are evil forces out there that are bent on dominating us. They want to separate us from God and others and isolate us, tearing us away from our place of belonging in the family of the Church. Those forces are nothing compared with the refuge that Christ provides for us, but we must also be intentional about taking refuge against our foe. The Church helps us to remember that and to act on it as we receive Holy Communion.

When we return to the image of a refuge, we realize that we must not only let Him enter under our roof, as we will pray together before receiving Communion, but we must also enter under *His* roof, fulfilling Christ's prayer to the Father as He instituted these Sacred Mysteries (see John 17). As expressed in that prayer of the great High Priest, this act of mutual, indwelling communion is a powerful force for evangelization, that the world may believe:

> Even as thou, Father, art in me, and I in thee, that they also may be in us, so that the world may believe that thou hast sent me. The glory which thou hast given me I have given to them, that they may be one even as we are one, I

in them and thou in me, that they may become perfectly one, so that the world may know that thou hast sent me and hast loved them even as thou hast loved me. (John 17:21–23)

Our Guardian for eternal life

When we receive the Body and Blood of Christ, we fix our attention on eternal life. Eternal life is not just an endless extension of this life. Pope Benedict XVI develops this point beautifully in his encyclical *Spe Salvi*, on Christian hope. He notes how hope drives us toward a life that is not threatened by death, a true life that is full of happiness and yet is something unknown because it is clearly different from the life we have now. He writes: "The term 'eternal life' is intended to give a name to this known 'unknown.'" Drawing from St. Augustine, he then elaborates:

> "Eternal", in fact, suggests to us the idea of something interminable, and this frightens us; "life" makes us think of the life that we know and love and do not want to lose, even though very often it brings more toil than satisfaction, so that while on the one hand we desire it, on the other hand we do not want it. To imagine ourselves outside the temporality that imprisons us and in some way to sense that eternity is not an unending succession of days in the calendar, but something more like the supreme moment of satisfaction, in which totality embraces us and we embrace totality—this we can only attempt. It would be like plunging into the ocean of infinite love, a moment in which time—the before and after—no longer exists. We can only attempt to grasp the idea that such a moment is life in the full sense, a plunging ever anew into the vastness of being,

in which we are simply overwhelmed with joy. This is how Jesus expresses it in Saint John's Gospel: "I will see you again and your hearts will rejoice, and no one will take your joy from you" (16:22). (12)

When it is described in this way, we see more clearly what we are tasting when we consume the Body and Blood of Christ. We are sacramentally touching that "supreme moment of satisfaction." We are dipping our hearts into that "ocean of infinite love." At that moment our longing expands even more, and at the same time, we feel our fragility. How easily we could lose this. We are capable of abandoning that very thing for which our whole life is so desperately aching.

It is for this reason that the Church places the gentle plea "*custodiat me*" on the lips of the priest at this precious moment of Holy Communion: "May the Body of Christ keep me safe for eternal life.... May the Blood of Christ keep me safe for eternal life."[152] We beg the Lord to stabilize and protect our wavering hearts. How easily we descend from this supreme moment of intimate love in receiving the Body and Blood of our Lord into the most mundane and even profane thoughts. How often do our hearts fail to respond with appropriate sentiments to the unbelievable gift that the Lord entrusts to us in this Sacrament Most Holy?

We can find some consolation in imagining the mixed affections of the apostles at that first Eucharist, before Christ died. Surely their hearts were filled with all the natural admixture of

---

[152] In the Latin original, the prayers are "Corpus Christi custodiat me in vitam aeternam.... Sanguis Christi custodiat me in vitam aeternam."

human feelings: confusion, uncertainty, intensity, intimacy, fear, hope, and a variety of thoughts ranging from logistics and control to trust and surrender. Perhaps they had anger at the mention of betrayal or envy over their relative position in their group. And we know these vices often mix with hope, faith, attention, love, and tenderness. We priests remain like them, human in the fragility of our hearts, but the Church helps us gently to refocus on what we are doing: "May the Body of Christ keep me safe for eternal life."

In addition to the beauty and intimacy of this moment of Holy Communion, the plea "*custodiat me*" — keep me safe, protect me, be my Guardian — also captures the ongoing journey of the Christian life. We need ongoing protection as we make our way through the remainder of the Mass and, after Mass, as we strive to lead a Christian life. We need our Guardian to keep us safe in the difficulties that inevitably await us and in the muddy paths that we must navigate. As St. John Henry Newman beautifully expressed it: "Lead, Kindly Light, amidst the encircling gloom. Lead Thou me on." The Body and Blood of Christ are the kindly light that leads us on.

We navigate our path by the substantial Presence of God that the Body and Blood bring into our souls and also by the divine logic they hold before our minds. The only secure path in this life is the way of Eucharistic love. The Body and Blood of Christ hold before us the safe way of the Cross — that is to say, the way of radical, self-emptying, self-sacrificing love. We do well to remember at this point the words of our Lord that call us on: "The gate is narrow and the way is hard, that leads to life, and those who find it are few" (Matt. 7:14). Our Lord speaks of the gate of Eucharistic love, the way of the Cross. He calls us to follow Him on the way that leads to life: "May the Body of Christ keep us safe for eternal life."

Contemplative silence

By reflecting on the priest's silent prayers in the Communion Rite, the faithful are guided into the silence of transcendence as they receive Holy Communion. Communion with God in the Body and Blood of Christ is a moment of supreme satisfaction, a plunging into the ocean of infinite love, a refuge from evil, freedom from sin, hope for new life, and a light for our path, as we elaborated in the last sections. Every communicant encounters God in a way that cannot be fully expressed in words. It is the silence of transcendence in which the communicant is steadily transformed into Christ, made one with His heart, His mind, and His will.

The silence of transcendence is a place of intimacy beyond the limits of words. Words are able to open doors into realities greater than the words can fully express. Symbolic words like the ritual texts, combined with the symbolic gestures of the liturgy, likewise point to the transcendent. The words of the Mass are able to make those transcendent realities truly present, by God's grace. In adoring those realities and entering into communion, words simply no longer suffice. This is the transcendent silence of adoration and communion.

Pope Francis identifies the presence of the Holy Spirit in the silence: "Liturgical silence is … a symbol of the presence and action of the Holy Spirit who animates the entire action of the celebration. For this reason it constitutes a point of arrival within a liturgical sequence. Precisely because it is a symbol of the Spirit, it has the power to express the Spirit's multifaceted action."[153] While the consecrated bread and wine are the Real Presence of Christ, the Holy Spirit comes to us in a particular way in the silence. It is in silence at the Elevation of the Eucharist that the Holy Spirit

---

[153] Pope Francis, *Desiderio Desideravi* 52.

moves in us in faith and love to adore the Lord Jesus. It is in the point of arrival at the silence of Holy Communion when the Holy Spirit brings us into a living union with Christ.

When addressing the International Theological Commission, Pope Benedict XVI illustrated this concept of encountering a reality beyond words as he narrated an episode in the life of St. Thomas Aquinas. As great as our words are, even when they use the words of God in Sacred Scripture and the inspired theology of the Catholic Church, they still fall short of the fullness of the reality we come into contact with in God:

> We are silent before the grandeur of God, for it dwarfs our words. This makes me think of the last weeks of St Thomas' life. In these last weeks, he no longer wrote, he no longer spoke. His friends asked him: "Teacher, why are you no longer speaking? Why are you not writing?" And he said: "Before what I have seen now all my words appear to me as straw".
>
> Fr Jean-Pierre Torrel, the great expert on St Thomas, tells us not to misconstrue these words. Straw is not nothing. Straw bears grains of wheat and this is the great value of straw. It bears the ear of wheat. And even the straw of words continues to be worthwhile since it produces wheat.
>
> For us, however, I would say that this is a relativization of our work; yet, at the same time, it is an appreciation of our work. It is also an indication in order that our way of working, our straw, may truly bear the wheat of God's Word.[154]

---

[154] Pope Benedict XVI, Homily at a Eucharistic Concelebration with the Members of the International Theological Commission.

The Hidden Power of Silence in the Mass

In addition to demonstrating the silence of transcendence in which even one of the greatest theologians, St. Thomas Aquinas, ultimately found himself, Pope Benedict XVI also describes how our writings and reflections can be more fruitful by drawing others into that space. When we find ways to reflect and witness to our own experience and deepening knowledge of God, we can help draw others into that communion with Christ which will bring them to the silence of transcendence.

At first, this sounds counterintuitive because there is always something radically personal about such profound, intimate encounters. At the same time, an episode from the life of St. Benedict draws out the possibility of sharing transcendence. Late in his life, St. Benedict had a vision and beheld the whole world in a single ray of light. St. Gregory, his biographer, explained:

> The light of holy contemplation enlarges and expands the mind in God until it stands above the world. In fact, the soul that sees Him rises even above itself, and as it is drawn upward in His light all its inner powers unfold. Then, when it looks down from above, it sees how small everything really is that was beyond its grasp before.[155]

There is much that could be said about St. Benedict's vision, but one remarkable thing was his urge to share this experience as he was having the vision:

> Wishing to have someone else witness this great marvel, he called out for Servandus, repeating his name two or

---

[155] Pope St. Gregory the Great, *The Life and Miracles of Saint Benedict: Book Two of the Dialogorum Libri Quatuor*, ed. the Benedictine Monks of Subiaco (Subiaco, Italy: Tipografia Editrice Santa Scholastica, 2023), 93.

three times in a loud voice. As soon as he heard the saint's call, Servandus rushed to the upper room and was just in time to catch a final glimpse of the miraculous light. He remained speechless with wonder as Benedict described everything that had taken place.[156]

The possibility of sharing a vision of transcendence is a particularly Christian desire. Knowing that we are made for communion, that it is not good for man to be alone, the Christian does not greedily gather up personal experiences but always wants to share the riches of grace with others. St. Benedict provides a wonderful example of how the heart of a saint desires to share the experience of transcendence.

This silence of transcendence could also be called a contemplative silence. It is the silence that comes from receiving the gift of God, which is the gift of Himself. In that gift, more words would spoil the moment. The *Catechism* describes the simplified prayer of gift, communion, and covenant as contemplative prayer:

> Contemplative prayer is the simplest expression of the mystery of prayer. It is a *gift*, a grace; it can be accepted only in humility and poverty. Contemplative prayer is a *covenant* relationship established by God within our hearts (cf. Jer. 31:33). Contemplative prayer is a *communion* in which the Holy Trinity conforms man, the image of God, "to his likeness." (2713)

The philosopher Bernard Dauenhauer, in his analysis of silence, calls this "deep silence." He identifies two other forms of silence related to the beginning and ending of words. Whereas the other

---

[156] Ibid., 91.

two forms of silence are related directly to the words they are shaping, this "deep silence" communicates without words:

> We engage in deep silence, for example, in discourse with intimates; in liturgy, where there is "someone," if not exactly another self; and in our normative sense of that which remains "to be said," that is, that which would ideally answer to, and thus authenticate our claims.[157]

The *Catechism* adds theological depth and richness to this philosophical reflection by adding the imagery of the fire of love. Furthermore, the *Catechism* provides an additional insight into how the silence of transcendence can gently be sustained:

> Contemplative prayer is *silence*, the "symbol of the world to come"[158] or "silent love."[159] Words in this kind of prayer are not speeches; they are like kindling that feeds the fire of love. In this silence, unbearable to the "outer" man, the Father speaks to us his incarnate Word, who suffered, died, and rose; in this silence the Spirit of adoption enables us to share in the prayer of Jesus. (2717)

The *Catechism* suggests that the contemplative fire of silent love can be gently sustained through words tossed in like kindling. This gives a direction for remaining in that place of communion and helps bring together a movement that might have begun early in the Mass. While feeling the transcendent silence of love in communion, one's

---

157 Williams, "Review of *Silence*," 237.

158 Cf. St. Isaac of Nineveh, *Tract. myst.* 66.

159 St. John of the Cross, *Maxims and Counsels*, 53 in *The Collected Works of St. John of the Cross*, tr. K. Kavanaugh, OCD, and O. Rodriguez, OCD (Washington, DC: Institute of Carmelite Studies, 1979), 678.

mind might start to wander. The fire of love might be gently renewed at that moment through recalling a word or image from earlier in the Mass. Perhaps through remembering a word of initial encounter from the Gospel or an image from the Offertory or a glimpse in the imagination during Holy Communion, the communicant can stir up the flame of union that has been set in the heart.

For example, one can imagine the interior path of a young man through the first four phases of silence. First, an initial silence of preparation exposed a particular insecurity that was hidden beneath the preoccupations of busyness in the man's heart. With that area of the heart exposed, he opened his attention to the Liturgy of the Word and heard the parable of the talents. For the first time, he recognized the generosity of the Master, who trusted him enough to share all his possessions with him and the other servants. Although he might have been tempted by fear of failure on a previous occasion, this time the silence of encounter led him to a deeper self-offering. He was able to lay down his many talents in the Lord's service and recommit himself to sharing the gifts he had received. At the same time, he was able to offer his painful insecurities as the priest placed incense on the charcoal. This led him to continue his offering in the Eucharistic Prayer and moved him to the silence of transcendence as he beheld and adored the Eucharistic Lord, elevated in His Body and Blood. Finally, as he received Holy Communion, he entered into a deeper silent intimacy, with love gently burning in his heart. As he remained there, he stoked the love with little remembrances of the Master, with little words in his heart whispering, "So generous, He trusts me so much …" Also, the tugging of his insecurities moved him to renew his offering through the incense, placing them again on the coal for worship. These examples of kindling the fire of love in his heart show us how the movements of silent prayer can work together in the Eucharist.

Although the silence of transcendence is a gift, we do have a choice as to how we respond to it. We can respond with surrender and let the gift bring us beyond our control to a place of silence, or we can respond by pulling back into our own control through exerting our skepticism and closing our hearts. Dauenhauer called this the "final cut" or "terminal silence":

> [There is] a "final cut," which he calls "terminal silence".... Such terminal silence ... may well send us back to perception, no less than direct us toward translinguistic insight. Indeed, the one is the terminal silence of the sceptic, the other, of the mystic. Or perhaps it may be by turns sceptical and mystical."[160]

When we let our communion with the Lord bring us into "translinguistic insight," we can find ourselves in the place of St. Thomas Aquinas: no longer able to express what is happening. This can make an intelligent man or woman feel very uncomfortable and even reduced to a more childlike state, unable to find words to capture the moment. Our letting go of the urge for control, however, is precisely what makes us ready for Heaven: "Truly, I say to you, unless you turn and become like children, you will never enter the kingdom of heaven. Whoever humbles himself like this child, he is the greatest in the kingdom of heaven" (Matt. 18:3–4).

Learning contemplative silence

Mary's example

There is a kind of silence that comes about because words fail. This is the contemplative silence of encountering transcendence. We can see this in Mary, as Pope Francis observed simply and

---

[160] Williams, "Review of *Silence*," 238.

beautifully about her: "*She speaks little, listens a lot, and cherishes in her heart* (cf. Lk 2:19)."[161] Her cherishing is in silence. She has learned to cherish the mystery of her Son in silence. It is beyond words. Who could put words to what happens in her after she makes her offering to God in the presence of the angel?

"Only in silence can the word of God find a home in us, as it did in Mary, woman of the word and, inseparably, woman of silence. Our liturgies must facilitate this attitude of authentic listening: *Verbo crescente, verba deficiunt.*"[162] The Latin phrase, taken from a sermon of St. Augustine, states that as the Word increases, our words fail. Our words are deficient to express what is happening as the Word of God grows in us—as we come before Him in adoration or receive Him in Holy Communion.

Mary is repeatedly stupefied, reduced to silent adoration and wonder. After the shepherds come, she is amazed (Luke 2:18). At the words of Simeon, she marvels (Luke 2:33). She is amazed at what Jesus says to the teachers in the Temple (Luke 2:47), and she does not understand what He says to her after she finds Him (Luke 2:50). In all of it, she simply remains with Him, adoring Him and continuing in communion with Him. She is a great example for us, both in her openness to amazement and her willingness to remain in that amazement without trying to resolve it into words or understanding.

Learning from St. Benedict

As mentioned earlier, at the end of his life, St. Benedict beheld the whole world in a single ray of light. This contemplative moment was the profound grace that he anticipated in the prologue of his

---

[161] Pope Francis, General Audience, Catechesis on Discernment 14.
[162] Pope Benedict XVI, *Verbum Domini* 66.

Rule when he admonished his followers: "Let us open our eyes to the light that comes from God" (RB, prologue 9). St. Benedict's experience was described eloquently by St. Gregory the Great:

> Long before the night office began, the man of God [St. Benedict] was standing at his window, where he watched and prayed while the rest were asleep. In the dead of night he suddenly beheld a flood of light shining down from above more brilliant than the sun, and with it every trace of darkness cleared away. Another remarkable sight followed. According to his own description, the whole world was gathered up before his eyes in what appeared to be a single ray of light.[163]

As mentioned earlier, St. Benedict saw, in a single glimpse, more than could be put into words, and so he thought it urgent to share it.

St. Benedict's impulse to share the experience is an inspiration for us who regularly encounter an equally magnificent or even more magnificent reality in the Mass. Our impulse, too, should be a desire to share this great mystery, knowing that we could never capture the experience in words.

The instruction of St. Benedict quoted above from the prologue of his Rule uses the phrase "*deificum lumen*" and could also be translated as "deifying light," so we could read it as: "Let us open our eyes to the deifying light." This light from God is also a light that transforms us more into God. The more we behold the deifying light of the Eucharist and receive from the divine light of the Sacred Mysteries of the altar, the more we are united to God, like the water in the wine. St. Benedict can continue

---

[163] Pope St. Gregory the Great, *The Life and Miracles of Saint Benedict*, 91.

to show us the way to encountering this light and to sharing it with others.

Practicing contemplative silence

Contemplative prayer is a grace that is received rather than a consequence of our initiatives. Of course, by setting the context, enkindling our desire for God, opening our hearts to the Lord, meditating on His Word, beholding His glory, and receiving His Body and Blood in Holy Communion, we maximize our possibility of encountering Him and receiving that grace of contemplative prayer. The one thing we can do to practice contemplative silence, however, is to remain in it. Having received the grace of contemplative prayer, we can choose to remain in it, not spoiling it with further words or actions, but simply allowing ourselves to enjoy our closeness to Him.

Furthermore, we can take advantage of the opportunities for silent adoration that have become exponentially more available in recent decades. By taking longer periods of time in prayer before the Blessed Sacrament, we can learn to renew our awe and wonder and to deepen our encounters with Christ. Over time, we can develop the ongoing loving attention to His presence that extends this grace of contemplative prayer throughout the regular activities of our lives. We learn to cultivate the holy desire that constitutes the basis for all prayer.

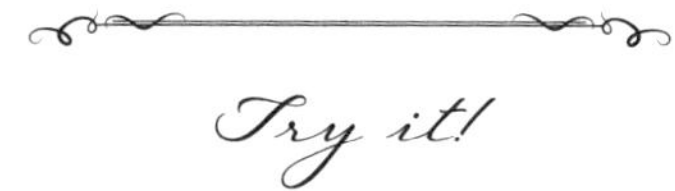

Try it!

Eucharistic adoration outside of Mass is one way to practice adoring the Lord in the Eucharist. The more time we spend in adoration of the Blessed Sacrament, the more powerful the moment will be when the priest elevates the Host and the chalice during the Mass. Try to spend an extra half hour in adoration of the Blessed Sacrament this week. During the time of adoration, look forward to the Elevation and Communion at Mass, imagining those moments and trying to enter into them more deeply. Then, at Mass, focus on those moments, building on your time in Eucharistic adoration. How did that exercise impact your experience? How could you improve it and build on it for the next time you attend Mass?

For further reflection

✠ In reflecting on God as the Mysterium tremendum et fascinans, how do you understand God as the Mysterium tremendum? Reflect on any experiences you have had of that. How do you understand Him as the Mysterium fascinans? Reflect on any experiences you have had of that.

✠ There are two prayers that the priest prays silently before receiving Holy Communion, and both have been used for approximately a thousand years. What comes to your mind and heart as you think about all the priests who have prayed those prayers in the Mass in the last thousand years? Is there a particular priest saint whom you admire? What is it like to imagine him praying one of those prayers? What is your favorite point or phrase from one of those prayers that you could bring into your own preparation for receiving the Eucharist?

✠ The Eucharist guards us for eternal life. What do you think of when you think of eternal life? Is that something you long for? Have you ever had a taste of eternity at Mass? What was it like?

✝ What is a contemplative silence? How can we understand that as a point of "arrival" in the Mass, as Pope Francis describes it? Describe an experience you have had with contemplative silence in your prayer or in the Mass. How could you or your parish cultivate more contemplative silence in the Mass?

✝ St. Benedict had a profound experience in prayer, and his first impulse was to share it. Have you ever wanted to share something profound that happened to you in prayer? Did you share it? How did that go? If you didn't share it, why not? What makes it hard to share our experiences of prayer?

6

Savoring in Silence (Eternal)

But the LORD is in his holy temple;
let all the earth keep silence before him.
(Hab. 2:20)

Following Holy Communion, the Roman Rite prescribes a period of private prayer: "When the distribution of Communion is over, if appropriate, the Priest and faithful pray quietly for some time. If desired, a Psalm or other canticle of praise or a hymn may also be sung by the whole congregation" (*GIRM* 88). If there is a hymn, it is in addition to the private prayer, and later the *GIRM* clarifies that this time after Holy Communion should include some period of silence: "After this, the priest may return to the chair. A sacred silence may now be observed for some time, or a Psalm or other canticle of praise or a hymn may be sung" (164). In fact, the *GIRM* uses a new adjective here, calling the silence "sacred." This silence has a special quality of savoring all that has taken place. Reminiscent of two lovers who share an intimate connection and rest in each other's presence, the Mass expects that after receiving the Body and Blood of Christ in a one-flesh union in Holy Communion, the communicant would also rest and savor this intimacy in a sacred silence. Here, silence plays a very different role than in the other periods. It is not preparing, not listening expectantly, not offering or touching transcendence. It is resting in the timelessness of the moment, savoring the eternal.

All of that is not to say that other interior movements of silence could not take place here — more listening, more self-offering, more transcendent encounter — but that it is at this point that the silence of savoring is most appropriate. Indeed, Cardinal Ratzinger writes: "This, in all truth, is the moment for an interior conversation with the Lord who has given himself to us, for that essential 'communicating,' that entry into the process of communication, without which the external reception of the Sacrament becomes mere ritual and therefore unfruitful."[164] Even the cardinal's use of the words *conversation* and *communication* here should not be taken in the sense of an information exchange but, rather, a mutual self-giving that aims at an intimate rest, as described by Christ using the image of the vine and the branches: "Abide in me, and I in you" (John 15:4).

There is a tendency to rush this sacred silence or omit it entirely, Ratzinger observes:

> Unfortunately, there are often hindrances that spoil this precious moment. The distribution of Communion continues with the noise of people going back and forth. In relation to the rest of the liturgical action, the distribution often lasts too long, which means that the priest feels the need to move the liturgy on quickly so that there is no empty period of waiting and restlessness, with people already getting ready to leave. Nevertheless, whenever

---

[164] Guardini and Ratzinger, *The Spirit of the Liturgy*, 224.

possible, this silence after Communion should be used, and the faithful should be given some guidance for interior prayer.[165]

The rush to end Mass is often driven by a sense of productivity. What is the use of just sitting there? There are things to accomplish. Sometimes there is an attitude that we have received what we came for and now we can get back to what is most important in life. To rush this sacred moment, however, is a grave mistake. Indeed, savoring the presence of God, especially when He is within us in Holy Communion, should extend even beyond the final blessing and dismissal in an act of thanksgiving, as will be discussed in a later section.

What is so important about this moment? It can be a time of healing. The rush to leave for the sake of greater productivity is part of a more widespread problem that Dr. Conrad Baars identified as energy neurosis, also connected with emotional deprivation. The Thomist Fr. Brian Mullady, O.P., explains: "There here are two basic desires in the passions. The one has to do with the good in itself—love, hate, desire, aversion, joy, sorrow; the other has to do with the good as something useful—hope, despair, courage, fear, and anger."[166] The passions (or emotions) related to usefulness can repress the passions (or emotions) related to the good in itself. This happens especially when a person has not been sufficiently emotionally affirmed—in other words, made to feel good in himself or herself. Sometimes a child is made to feel good only insofar as he or she is useful. Some people were forced into adult roles while still children and were never given permission

---

[165] Ibid.

[166] Brian Thomas Mullady, *St. Thomas Aquinas Rescues Modern Psychology* (Irondale, AL: EWTN Publishing, 2022), 55.

to enjoy childhood. Always driven forward, these people continue to drive themselves:

> The busy, driven man cannot be bothered with other people unless they can serve his own utilitarian goals which keep him on the go at all times. The man running through a museum cannot be moved by the beauty of the paintings and sculptures. To the gourmand who gulps his drinks and bolts his food, all foods taste the same. It is the quantity he is after, not quality. Only the contemplative person, the connoisseur of art, the gourmet are aware of the goodness of things, and being moved by this goodness, find joy and happiness. Quiet as well as silence is essential, too, for only the silent hear … what the other has to say. Only the quiet can perceive what the other reveals.[167]

Baars described the way that living in a rushed manner saps life of joy and happiness. For someone who is living this way—and Baars saw this as the most prevalent neurosis in the Western world, rapidly growing even in 1975, when his book *Born Only Once* was originally published[168]—the answer is not to shame oneself for not sitting still. Simply desiring to find peace by sitting still will not yield immediate results. The first point is to realize this is happening in one's life and then to begin exploring what might be driving it. In emotional deprivation, there is a lack of emotional affirmation. Baars uses *affirmation* in a technical sense to describe the firmness that comes from the

---

[167] Conrad W. Baars, *Born Only Once: The Miracle of Affirmation*, ed. Suzanne M. Baars and Bonnie N. Shayne, 3rd ed. (Eugene, OR: Wipf and Stock, 2016), 55.

[168] Ibid., 4.

loving attention of another person who makes one feel like a gift, simply by virtue of the fact of that person's existence. When one has the firm foundation of feeling that one is a gift, one can also begin to receive life and others as gifts. Then it is possible to enjoy the good in itself.

One thing we could meditate on after receiving the Body and Blood of Christ is the fact that we have been chosen. Christ has chosen to dwell in us and rest in us. He has chosen us because He enjoys us. He has not come to us because of all the good things we have done or because we have followed all the rules. He has chosen us and He rests in us because He loves us. From this perspective, we are not only enjoying His presence in Holy Communion, but in the sacred silence we are also letting Him enjoy our presence and the home He has made in our hearts. We allow for silence in order to let Him love us, simply for who we are.

For those who are driven to productivity, another encouragement can be found in the writings of St. Thérèse, as she interprets the teaching of St. John of the Cross: "O my Jesus! I love You! I love the Church, my Mother! I recall that '*the smallest act of PURE LOVE is of more value to her than all other works together.*'"[169] St. Thérèse understands and expresses emphatically the inestimable value of loving Jesus. There is nothing more important that we can accomplish than this act of pure love. Furthermore, the closeness that we have to Jesus in sacramental Communion is of the highest magnitude, so the opportunity to love Him in this moment deserves at least a few minutes of sacred silence.

---

[169] St. Thérèse of Lisieux, *Story of a Soul: Study Edition*, ed. Marc Foley, trans. John Clarke (Washington, DC: ICS Publications, 2005), 305. St. Thérèse quotes from St. John of the Cross's *Spiritual Canticle*, stanza 29, no. 2.

Purification of the vessels includes our hearts

The final quiet prayer of the priest is offered while he purifies the sacred vessels after Holy Communion: "What has passed our lips as food, O Lord, may we possess in purity of heart, that what has been given to us in time may be our healing for eternity.[170] The prayer's origin is ancient, already found in the earliest sacramentaries.[171] The indication was always that it was to be said quietly, and so it is intended to be the personal prayer of the priest. At the same time, it uses the plural, and in some ancient sacramentaries, it is coupled with instructions that it be said after all have finished receiving Communion.[172] Thus, although the priest is praying privately, it is not self-centered but is still communal in its intention.

In the 1962 missal, we also find the prayer Corpus Tuum, Domine translated roughly as "May Your Body, O Lord, which I have received, and Your Blood which I have drunk, cleave to my innermost being; and grant that no stain of sin may remain in me, who have been fed with this pure and holy Sacrament; Who lives and reigns for ever and ever. Amen." This prayer, although going back only to the ninth century, is worth including here because of its publication in the eleventh-century *Communion Devotions of Monte Cassino*, where it was provided for the devotional use of the faithful.[173] As mentioned earlier, these prayers can assist the faithful as well as the priest in entering more deeply into the Mass. This prayer expresses particularly beautifully the way the Blessed Sacrament cleaves to the deepest parts of us. We sometimes say

---

[170] In Latin, the prayer is "Quod ore sumpsimus, Domine, pura mente capiamus: et de munere temporali fiat nobis remedium sempiternum."

[171] Jungmann, *The Mass of the Roman Rite*, 2:400.

[172] Ibid., 401.

[173] Ibid.

that a hearty, sustaining food "sticks to our ribs." Analogously, the Blessed Sacrament sticks to our souls.

To focus now on the prayer for the purification of the vessels provided in the missal of Paul VI, we see that a central theme of the prayer is an ongoing possession of the sacrament with purity. *Purity* is a rich word in our Catholic Faith that sometimes wrongly takes on narrowly moralistic tones or even evokes Puritan connotations of dour and joyless dispositions. To the contrary, St. John Henry Newman saw purity as being intimately connected with love: "Purity prepares the soul for love, and love confirms the soul in purity."[174] The *Catechism* expands on this explanation of purity by including truth and chastity: " 'Pure in heart' refers to those who have attuned their intellects and wills to the demands of God's holiness, chiefly in three areas: charity (cf. 1 Tim. 4:3–9; 2 Tim. 2:22); chastity or sexual rectitude (cf. 1 Thess. 4:7; Col. 3:5; Eph. 4:19); love of truth and orthodoxy of faith (cf. Titus 1:15; 1 Tim. 1:3–4; 2 Tim 2:23–26). There is a connection between purity of heart, of body, and of faith" (2518). We can easily see how this richer understanding of purity could be connected with reception of the Bread of Angels. We want every reception of Holy Communion to enlighten our minds with truth, like the minds of the angels, and deepen our bodily integrity even as it enflames our hearts with love.

We can also think of purity in terms of pure spring water. In this way, we see how it implies a clarity, transparency, and lack of duplicity. Pure spring water is not discolored, and it does not have any debris or anything else mixed in it. This describes very well the purity that we pray for in receiving Holy Communion.

---

[174] John Henry Newman, *Discourses Addressed to Mixed Congregations* (London: Longmans, Green, 1906), 63.

We want to be the same throughout our whole self. When we are at Mass or receiving Holy Communion, we rightly try to be at our best. This is true especially for a priest, who is most truly a priest, and thus should be most truly himself, in the celebration of the Eucharist.

The ongoing work of the Christian life is to spread our best throughout the whole of our lives. According to Bl. Abbot Columba Marmion, the keynote of the Rule of Benedict is that the divine presence is everywhere. St. Benedict essentially arranges every dimension of the monastic life to help the monk tune in to the divine presence everywhere. But he says that we should be especially aware of the divine presence when we celebrate the liturgy (RB 19:1). Such authenticity and integrity is a fruit of our effort and a fruit of grace. It is particularly appropriate to pray for this grace, then, especially at this privileged moment when the living Flesh and Blood of the Incarnate Lord is alive in us sacramentally.

Also in these moments shortly after receiving Holy Communion, we are positioned between Heaven and Earth, and so we end this prayer after Communion asking "that what has been given to us in time may be our healing for eternity." We are still in the heavenly realm of the Eucharistic Prayer and the Communion Rite. At the same time, we are very much on Earth in our humanity. We are tasting eternity in communing with the Eternal One, while also possibly feeling the pressures of time as we draw close to the end of the Mass. We do well to savor these moments of eternity as we pray that the medicine (the literal translation is "remedy") of the Eucharist may stir up hope in us for Heaven and do its work on our hearts to help us get there.

This is the silence of savoring. In our savoring of the encounter with God in the Word and the contemplative graces we receive in Holy Communion, we taste a little of Heaven, and we rightly linger there as the healing power of the Sacrament flows through us. Drawing on this image of healing, with the grace of the consumed Sacrament seeking out the areas of our souls that are in need, there is a striking analogy in the biological realm. The recent discoveries with adult-stem-cell treatments provide a powerful image for how healing can take place in the body, and we can envision a similar process in the soul. When the physical heart is damaged through a heart attack, scar tissue inhibits heart function. Stem cells drawn from a healthy part of a person's own body can be used to heal that scar tissue. It's only necessary for the stem cells to be prepared and then injected near the site of the damage. The stem cells then seek out the damaged heart tissue and begin to regenerate new, healthy tissue.[175]

The analogy to the Eucharist is in the way that the living Body of Jesus can bring healing to the scarred areas of our souls. Received in faith, the Eucharist acts like stem cells, regenerating life in the areas of our hearts that we allow our Lord to enter. Many times, this starts with an initial response of trust from a healthy part of our faith life (like drawing forth stem cells from a healthy part of the body). Then, in our prayer, we apply that encounter with Jesus to a damaged or diseased part. In bringing the healthy together with the sick, the sick is healed. We can imagine this taking place as we savor in silence the communion we have experienced with Jesus in the Eucharist. We can invite Him or at least allow Him to seek out the places in us that are damaged or diseased. We can savor the touch of His love in the most tender places in our hearts.

---

[175] Louis A. Cona, "Stem Cell Therapy for Heart Failure," *Stem Cell Blog by DVC*, April 24, 2023, https://www.dvcstem.com/post/stem-cells-reverse-heart-disease.

The Hidden Power of Silence in the Mass

Maronite farewell prayer to the altar

In our meditation after receiving Communion, one prayer that can
provide some inspiration is the silent prayer after the final blessing
in the celebration of the Eucharist in the Maronite Rite (in fact, it
is the only prayer in the Maronite Rite that is supposed to be prayed
silently after the start of the liturgy). It has the sweetness of savoring,
expressing a special love for the altar on which the Eucharistic sacrifice
has just taken place. The altar is indeed the symbol of Christ (CCC
1383), and it symbolizes many central features of the Lord's mysteries:

> The *altar* of the New Covenant is the Lord's Cross (cf. Heb.
> 13:10), from which the sacraments of the Paschal mystery
> flow. On the altar, which is the center of the church, the
> sacrifice of the Cross is made present under sacramental
> signs. The altar is also the table of the Lord, to which the
> People of God are invited. In certain Eastern liturgies, the
> altar is also the symbol of the tomb (Christ truly died and
> is truly risen). (CCC 1182)

These symbols are borne out in the Maronite Rite with this prayer
of final veneration for the altar. Truly, it is a prayer of tender love,
indicating the special relationship that the priest has with the altar,
but it also guides the faithful to think about their relationship to
the altar in particular and to the whole church building where
their Eucharistic encounter with the Lord takes place. Taking time
at the end of Mass to savor all the elements that have supported,
housed, and presented the sacred mysteries of Christ's life, death,
and Resurrection is a worthy way to savor in silence.

As he kisses the altar, the priest prays silently:

> I leave you in peace, O holy Altar, and I hope to return to
> you in peace. May the offering I have received from you be

for the forgiveness of my faults and the remission of my sins, that I may stand without shame or fear before the throne of Christ. I do not know if I shall be able to return to you again to offer another sacrifice. I leave you in peace.

The notes of peace and the reiteration of the centermost effects of the liturgy (forgiveness of faults, remission of sins, and the ability to stand before God without shame or fear) make up the heart of this prayer. These effects should not be forgotten as those who have received Christ are now called to go forth and serve Him in love. That loving service calls them, purified by the forgiveness of their sins, actively to engage in the world while remaining in a loving posture before the throne of God. Indeed, the Lord is now enthroned in the hearts of the believers in a particularly powerful way.

The unique sentiments of the prayer involve the initial expressions of affection for the altar, acknowledging the sorrow of departure and the hope of return. After savoring what has taken place in the Mass, a tender affection develops in the heart that resists separation. Although the Eucharist is only for this life and will give way to vision in the life to come, we develop a deep affection for these sacred rituals. They become a comfort, a shelter, a refuge for us while we are wayfaring toward our heavenly home.

There is also the expression of how the altar has provided the offering. The altar is not merely a piece of furniture; it becomes deeply intertwined with the Eucharistic sacrifice. The sense of the prayer is that the altar has helped us on our journey to be purified of sin and to stand without shame or fear before the throne of Christ. The altar is a friend of the priest, who has placed his hands on it, leaned on it, and placed on it the most sacred treasure of the Eucharist and all the sacred vessels. Especially when a priest celebrates Mass every day at the altar in his parish church, he develops a deep connection with the altar, as do the faithful who come to Mass every day and look at the altar from which will come their daily Bread.

This prayer fosters the silence of savoring. As the priest prays silently, the faithful also savor this bittersweet moment at the end of Mass. It is sweet for all that has unfolded in the re-presentation of God's love. It is bitter for having ended, especially without certainty that it will ever take place again. Just as it is helpful to enter into Mass with the attitude of its being the first, last, and only Mass one might attend, so it is helpful to end the Mass with the same sentiment. Indeed, this Mass will never be repeated since each celebration has its own uniqueness. Something great and beautiful has taken place, and we should savor it as we depart, conscious that "I do not know if I shall be able to return to you again to offer another sacrifice."

Thanksgiving After Mass

Although the Mass provides some brief times of silence for savoring the graces of Communion, there is more to be savored that can extend into the period after Mass. This time of thanksgiving after Mass is not specifically prescribed, as are the various silences or private prayers during Mass. The only prescription, in fact, comes through canon law, rather than through the *GIRM*. Canon 909 reads: "A priest is not to neglect to prepare himself properly through prayer for the celebration of the eucharistic sacrifice and to offer thanks to God at its completion."

What precisely does this thanksgiving consist of? In a section titled "Thanksgiving after Mass" in the missal of Paul VI, we find some prayers that are also found in the 1962 missal. The collection in the more recent missal is somewhat reduced, but it still contains the prayer of St. Thomas Aquinas ("I give thanks to Thee, O Lord …"), the Anima Christi, the prayer of St. Ignatius of Loyola ("Receive Lord, my entire freedom …"), the Prayer before a Crucifix, ("Behold, O good and loving Jesus …"), the Universal Prayer attributed to Pope Clement XI ("I believe, O Lord, but may I believe more firmly …"), and prayers to the Blessed Virgin Mary. Clearly, these prayers could be used to satisfy the canonical requirement.

We should, however, consider the thanksgiving after Mass, required by the *Code of Canon Law* for the priest—and surely just as important for the faithful—to be more than a few more prayers to be recited. The Church's law is providing us with some spiritual direction in this case. Even after the liturgical prayers have ended, personal prayer has not ended. In fact, these moments following the liturgical prayer are particularly fruitful for continued personal prayer. This is a time for savoring the graced moments of the Mass.

In former times, some prayers for particular intentions were prescribed during this special time immediately after Mass. Pope Leo XIII's prayers after a Low Mass fit into this category and build on a prayer for the liberation of the Church that was prescribed by Bl. Pius IX. At other times in history, as well, prayers were added immediately after Mass for special intentions that were local, regional, or universal.[176] The intuition is that this time immediately after Mass has a special efficacy and that important intentions should be lifted up to God while He is still so close to us in the communal celebration of the Sacred Mysteries.

One special intention that we should always have is that the Eucharist we have just celebrated will have the greatest possible fruitfulness in our souls. This is the sense of the Prayer of St. Thomas Aquinas, which includes phrases such as: "May [this Holy

---

[176] Jungmann, *The Mass of the Roman Rite*, 2:455–456.

Communion] cancel my faults, destroy concupiscence and carnal passion, increase charity and patience, humility and obedience, and all the virtues." Following the Mass, we also anticipate the challenges and trials we will face as we go out into the world, and so we pray for protection: "May it be a firm defense against the snares of all my enemies, both visible and invisible."

The Anima Christi leads us into an intimate union with Christ, reflecting the realism of the sacramental encounter that has just taken place. The Eucharist is no mere symbol!

> Soul of Christ, sanctify me.
> Body of Christ, save me.
> Blood of Christ, inebriate me.
> Water from Christ's side, wash me.
> Passion of Christ, strengthen me.
> O good Jesus, hear me.
> Within Thy wounds hide me.
> Suffer me not to be separated from Thee.
> From the malicious enemy defend me.
> In the hour of my death call me
> And bid me come unto Thee
> That I may praise Thee with Thy saints
> and with Thy angels
> Forever and ever. Amen.

In the Anima Christi, we ask for the salvation that comes from Christ's Body, the inebriation that comes from His Blood, the strength that comes from His Passion, the safe refuge that can be found by entering into His Wounds, and the sanctification that comes from our encounter with His soul. The Byzantines offer very expressive prayers during the Mass in preparation for receiving Holy Communion. Although we do not do that in the Roman

Rite during the Mass, the Anima Christi, which can be offered in thanksgiving, reflects back with a particularly vivid description of the kind of tender, human-divine encounter that takes place in Holy Communion. Following the Mass, it is an especially meaningful and appropriate prayer to offer so that our intimate union with Christ, given in the grace of Holy Communion, may extend into the rest of our lives.

The Prayer of Self-Offering by St. Ignatius and the Prayer before the Crucifix do not reflect the reception of Holy Communion as directly, but they still personalize the encounter that takes place in the Mass and extend that encounter into our lives. These words of surrender and our placing ourselves before our Lord's gaze properly and concisely capture the attitude that should remain in us as we end our celebration of the Sacred Mysteries. These are movements of savoring, and they extend into moments of silence. The Universal Prayer attributed to Pope Clement XI, on the other hand, seems to cover all possible needs of our souls. It will be remembered more for its comprehensive content than for its brevity! The final prayer offered in the missal is to the Blessed Virgin Mary, and it tenderly speaks of the reality of receiving her Son in Holy Communion and asks her to help us not to waste this unbelievable gift.

Each of these prayers gives us a sense of the attitude we want to cultivate in our hearts following the Mass. This is directly contrary to the attitude of efficiency that can reduce the Mass to a function and measures it only by the quantity of time it takes. The intuition of lovers is to linger a little longer with the beloved. We may do that with these prayers provided in the missal, but there is also an ancient practice of entering into a little meditation while we are still in the glow of the Eucharistic celebration.

The liturgical historian Fr. Josef Jungmann, S.J., beautifully describes this special time of thanksgiving following the Mass: "Next comes silent prayer and meditation. It is no discovery of modern piety that the time after Mass and Communion, when the crowd has dispersed and quiet has settled over the church, is a time for the priest—and the same holds for the faithful—to give himself to more than vocal prayer."[177] The Passionist tradition established by St. Paul of the Cross regulated thirty minutes of meditation before Mass and thirty minutes after Mass. Prior to St. Paul of the Cross, this was already promoted in *The Imitation of Christ*.[178]

All of this is to say that there is a minimum requirement to make some thanksgiving after Mass, rather than to rush immediately out the door and on to the next activity. The invitation to thanksgiving does not prescribe minimums, and so we should seek to follow this direction in a generous way and resist the temptation to fall into a minimalism. The generous heart will remain a little longer with the Beloved following the celebration of the source and summit of our Faith. That sweet time should be marked by tender expressions of love, acknowledging the realism of the encounter with Jesus Christ in His Body, Blood, Soul, and Divinity; asking for the graces to continue living the Eucharist in daily life; and, above all, meditating on what has happened as we rest in the presence of the Great Lover, who dwells a little longer in our bodies.

Learning eternal silence

Mary's example

Scripture tells us twice that Mary savors in silence. The first time is after the visit of the shepherds and their message about the angels' song of glory: "Mary kept all these things, pondering them in her heart" (Luke 2:19). The second time is after the finding

---

177 Ibid., 463.
178 Thomas à Kempis, *The Imitation of Christ*, bk. 4, chap. 1, no. 24.

of Jesus in the Temple: "His mother kept all these things in her heart" (Luke 2:51). In the first case, "kept" is a translation of the Greek *tereo*, and in the second case, it is a translation of the Greek word *diatereo*, which is the same root with an added prefix. In both cases, the verb indicates that Mary is keeping in the sense of guarding or treasuring. She is actively protecting what she has received and holding on to them in her heart. The way that she can collect these things and hold on to them in her heart gives us the sense of Mary's heart as a treasure house that is steadily filled with sacred mysteries. Her interior is not a grate through which these experiences simply drain out. Rather, she sorts and collects and continues to reflect on all that she has seen and heard, particularly in her direct experience of the Son of God.

In this way, she models for us how we can store up in our hearts our direct experience of the Son of God in the Mass. We have heard Him and beheld Him, and if we received Holy Communion, He has truly entered into our hearts. In the time of silence after Communion and continuing after Mass, we should keep these things in our hearts—we should guard them as a treasure and store them where they can continue to be part of our thoughts and our feelings as they guide our actions. In the chapter on encounter, we reflected on how Mary "ponders" these things, throwing them together (*symbállō*) with her life to understand the events more deeply and to understand her life more deeply in light of the events. This is dependent on first *keeping* the sacred mysteries in her heart. Then, over time, the extended reflection becomes a song of praise, a Magnificat!

Learning from St. Benedict

We already mentioned how St. Benedict admonished his monks to depart in silence from the oratory after completing the Divine

Office so that a brother might remain and pray alone without disturbance from the insensitivity of others (RB 52:2–3). This is good advice for our parish churches, cathedrals, and shrines as well. What a difference it makes when the church is in silence for those who wish to remain and pray after the Mass. It takes time, patience, and fatherly gentleness to steadily transform parish culture to foster such silences without introducing offenses against charity, such as harsh stares and shaming judgments. Each parishioner can contribute personal witness, however, by moving conversations in a kind way from the nave to the narthex.

In addition to fostering silence in the oratory in order to support personal prayer along with liturgical prayer in that dedicated space, St. Benedict supports the silence of savoring by encouraging the monks to cultivate the presence of God at all times. As mentioned earlier, what is considered the keynote that permeates the whole Rule is this: "We believe that the divine presence is everywhere" (RB 19:1). St. Benedict's teaching throughout the Holy Rule connects the various aspects in the monk's life to the divine presence, helping the monk to develop a constant, loving attention to that presence. St. Benedict builds that awareness on the standard of God's presence in the liturgy in the next verse of the Rule: "But beyond the least doubt we should believe this to be especially true when we celebrate the divine office" (RB 19:2). In other words, a monk's whole life could be considered an opportunity to savor the presence of God that was fundamentally experienced in the liturgy. It's no wonder St. Benedict urged monks to cultivate silence at all times (RB 42:1).

Practicing the silence of savoring

We can deepen our practice of savoring divine grace in silence in several ways. One way is to remain longer after Mass. Even dedicating a few minutes to silent prayers of thanksgiving, in order to rest in the Lord's presence, would start to give room for our hearts to grow. Returning to the insights of Dr. Conrad Baars presented earlier in this book, there would be a real benefit to healing and developing our humane emotions if we left more time just for being in church after Mass rather than running off to the next thing we must do.

At a nearby Passionist house of solitude in Bedford, Pennsylvania, the small Passionist community used to host forty-day retreats for men, mostly priests. The superior and founder of the house, Fr. Silvan Rouse, C.P., testified to the impact it made on the priests when they spent half-hour periods of silence in prayer before and after Mass. He said that that was the most common remark from the priests about the positive, lasting impact of the retreats. There are many reasons why we struggle to take such a significant amount of time for prayer before and after Mass. Although it may not be possible for every Mass or even most of the time, perhaps we can spend that lengthy period sometimes and see how it helps us develop a habit of savoring.

Likewise, in the spirit of the Maronite farewell prayer to the altar, we could actively reflect on the aspects of the church's interior that we love and take time to soak those in. Who knows if we will ever see them again? Also, after Mass, we could go over the Mass again in our minds. What were the readings? What struck our hearts? How did we offer ourselves? Where did we encounter God in the Mass? We can even journal some of these points, as long as we do not place that on ourselves as an additional burden or duty. In a related way, following the advice of St. Francis de Sales, we can save one of these words, images, or experiences in the Mass as a little flower that we place in our breast pocket and take with us for the rest of the day. We can sniff that flower by calling to mind the word or insight that was connected with our feeling of God's closeness. This has a way of fostering recollection, extending the grace of the Mass into the rest of the day, and helping us cultivate an ongoing savoring of God with a contemplative heart like our Lady's.

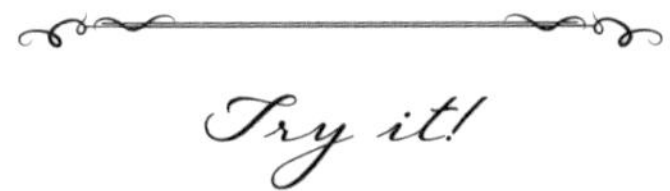

Try it!

For the next several Masses you attend, spend five minutes after Mass making a thanksgiving prayer. What is it like to linger a while after Mass to make a thanksgiving? Are you able to savor the presence of our Lord more deeply? How would you advise others to make a thanksgiving?

For further reflection

+ Dr. Conrad Baars encourages us to slow down and allow our feelings to engage reality more fully. There are good things that can be savored with joy. There are bad things that can be grieved with hurt and sadness. Both expand our hearts. We can practice slowing down and giving room for our feelings by the way we engage the Sacred Mysteries. What prevents you from slowing down? What things do you tend to rush off to after Mass? What are you afraid would happen if you slowed down and savored the experience?

+ The Maronite farewell prayer to the altar acknowledges that we may never return to Mass again. What is it like to think about never attending Mass again? Is that sad? Scary? How does it help you appreciate the Mass with greater gratitude?

✛ When St. Thérèse declares that "the smallest act of pure love is of more value to her [the Church] than all her other works together," how does that strike you? How does this statement affect your priorities? How does it change your view of others? How does it affect the way you approach the Mass?

✛ What does the phrase "purity of heart" make you think of? How did the explanation of purity in this chapter influence your ideas? How do you associate purity with the Eucharist?

Conclusion

Creation, Incarnation, and interior transformation all happen according to these five movements of silence: ascetical, mystical, sacrificial, contemplative, and eternal. In the liturgy of the Roman Rite, the Church has developed a ritual path by which the faithful can move through these five passages of silence and so be gradually transformed into Christ. Following the pattern of Creation and Incarnation, our interior transformation is brought about steadily through the liturgy by full, conscious, active participation, especially interiorly and particularly in silence. Furthermore, as the faithful are steadily transformed by the Eucharist, as the source, center, and summit of the Church's life, they, in turn, steadily transform the world. For this reason, the fruitful participation in the Eucharist—and, in a special way, in the silence of the Mass—can have a massive, global impact. This is nothing less than the power of the Cross extended throughout time and space, transforming everything into divine love.

This is the notion of liturgical formation promoted by Pope Francis, inspired by the statements of Pope St. Paul VI and Fr. Romano Guardini:

From all that we have said about the nature of the Liturgy it becomes clear that knowledge of the mystery of Christ, the decisive question for our lives, does not consist in a mental assimilation of some idea but in real existential engagement with his person. In this sense, Liturgy is not about "knowledge," and its scope is not primarily pedagogical, even though it does have great pedagogical value. (Cf. *Sacrosanctum Concilium*, n. 33) Rather, Liturgy is about praise, about rendering thanks for the Passover of the Son whose power reaches our lives. The celebration concerns the reality of our being docile to the action of the Spirit who operates through it until Christ be formed in us. (Cf. Gal 4:19) The full extent of our formation is our conformation to Christ. I repeat: it does not have to do with an abstract mental process, but with becoming Him. This is the purpose for which the Spirit is given, whose action is always and only to confect the Body of Christ. It is that way with the Eucharistic bread, and with every one of the baptized called to become always more and more that which was received as a gift in Baptism; namely, being a member of the Body of Christ. Leo the Great writes, "Our participation in the Body and Blood of Christ has no other end than to make us become that which we eat." [Leo Magnus, Sermo LXIII: *De Passione Domini* III, 7.][179]

Pope Francis describes powerfully how the liturgy is capable of transforming us into Christ. He notes the power of the Spirit, whose masterpiece is the Incarnation of Christ, and he notes how the Holy Spirit keeps repeating that greatest possible work in each

---

[179] Pope Francis, *Desiderio Desideravi* 41.

one of the baptized. The liturgy is wielded in power by the Holy Spirit for that transforming work. Culminating in the silence of Communion and extending into our lives through the eternal silence of His Presence in us, the work of the liturgy steadily transforms the world.

In light of this, it is understandable that Pope Francis lauded the Benedictines as he declared the impact of our love for and our celebration of the liturgy:

> Your love for the liturgy, which is the essential work of God in monastic life, is essential first and foremost for you yourselves, enabling you to abide in the living presence of the Lord; and it is valuable for the whole Church which, in the course of centuries has benefited from it as from spring water which irrigates and fertilizes, nourishing the capacity to experience, personally and in community, the encounter with the Risen Lord.[180]

The liturgy is valuable for the whole Church and fosters the personal and communal encounter with the risen Lord. That encounter happens especially in silence. Pope Francis further praised the Benedictines for the silence we cultivate in our monasteries and the healing power of that silence for bringing order and harmony to our interior lives, especially in today's busy world:

> In this era, in which people are so busy that they do not have enough time to listen to God's voice, your monasteries and your convents become as oases, where men and women of every age, origin, culture and religion can discover the

---

[180] Pope Francis, Address to the Monks of the Benedictine Confederation, April 19, 2018.

beauty of silence and rediscover themselves, in harmony with creation, allowing God to re-establish just order in their life.[181]

As Pope Francis noted, in silence we rediscover ourselves. At first, that can be a difficult experience, and the first movement of silence is understandably ascetical, even penitential, as in the beginning of the Mass. Soon, though, as we are able to make room inside ourselves and to open the ear of our hearts, we can encounter the Lord in His loving Word. Each encounter leads to a deeper surrender as we learn to open our whole hearts and bring our whole lives into relationship with God. This is especially hard in the areas of our limitations, our wounds, our aching, and our dying. This requires perseverance because there are places in our hearts that are uncovered only through changing circumstances and across longer stretches of time. As we persevere in faithfully attending Mass and participating fully, consciously, and actively, these newly opened areas are brought into this dynamic of encounter and self-offering. The Mass helps us, in silence, to bring our whole lives into relationship with God. This opens up steadily more as we grow in communion with Him and savor His loving presence in our souls.

We conclude with the inspiring words of Pope St. John Paul II in his last encyclical. As, in each chapter, we have looked to Mary and learned from St. Benedict, we have followed the itinerary sketched out for us by this great pope, who concludes with an act of silent adoration and unbounded love:

Let us take our place, dear brothers and sisters, *at the school of the saints*, who are the great interpreters of true Eucharistic piety. In them the theology of the Eucharist takes on

181 Ibid.

all the splendour of a lived reality; it becomes "contagious" and, in a manner of speaking, it "warms our hearts". Above all, let us *listen to Mary Most Holy*, in whom the mystery of the Eucharist appears, more than in anyone else, as a mystery of light. Gazing upon Mary, we come to know *the transforming power present in the Eucharist*. In her we see the world renewed in love. Contemplating her, assumed body and soul into heaven, we see opening up before us those "new heavens" and that "new earth" which will appear at the second coming of Christ. Here below, the Eucharist represents their pledge, and in a certain way, their anticipation: "*Veni, Domine Iesu!*" (Rev 22:20).

In the humble signs of bread and wine, changed into his body and blood, Christ walks beside us as our strength and our food for the journey, and he enables us to become, for everyone, witnesses of hope. If, in the presence of this mystery, reason experiences its limits, the heart, enlightened by the grace of the Holy Spirit, clearly sees the response that is demanded, and bows low in adoration and unbounded love.[182]

---

[182] Pope St. John Paul II, encyclical letter *Ecclesia de Eucharistia* (April 17, 2003), no. 62.

Bibliography

Acklin, Fr. Thomas, and Fr. Boniface Hicks. *Personal Prayer: A Guide for Receiving the Father's Love.* Steubenville, OH: Emmaus Road Publishing, 2020.

———. *Spiritual Direction: A Guide for Sharing the Father's Love.* Steubenville, OH: Emmaus Road Publishing, 2017.

Albacete, Lorenzo. *The Cry of the Heart: On the Meaning of Suffering.* Seattle: Slant Books, 2023.

Arminjon, Blaise. *The Cantata of Love: A Verse-by-Verse Reading of the Song of Songs.* San Francisco: Ignatius Press, 1988.

Athanasius, St. *Life of St. Anthony.* In *Early Christian Biographies,* edited by Roy Joseph Deferrari. Vol. 15 of The Fathers of the Church. Washington, DC: Catholic University of America Press, 1952.

Augustine of Hippo, St. *Confessions.* Edited by Roy Joseph Deferrari. Translated by Vernon J. Bourke. Vol. 21 of The Fathers of the Church. Washington, DC: Catholic University of America Press, 1953.

Baars, Conrad W. *Born Only Once: The Miracle of Affirmation.* Edited by Suzanne M. Baars and Bonnie N. Shayne. 3rd ed. Eugene, OR: Wipf and Stock, 2016.

———. *Feeling and Healing Your Emotions.* Edited by Suzanne M. Baars and Bonnie N. Shayne. Updated ed. Alachua, FL: Bridge-Logos, 2009.

Benedict, St. *RB 1980: The Rule of St. Benedict in Latin and English with Notes.* Edited by Timothy Fry. Collegeville, MN: Liturgical Press, 1981.

Benedict XVI, Pope. "Address to the Parish Priests and the Clergy of Rome," February 14, 2013.

———. Address to the Participants in the International Congress Organized to Commemorate the Fortieth Anniversary of the Dogmatic Constitution *Dei Verbum*, September 16, 2005.

———. General Audience. Catecheses on prayer, August 10, 2011; November 30, 2011; February 8, 2012.

———. Homily at the Closing Mass of World Youth Day at Marienfeld, Cologne, Germany, August 21, 2005.

———. Homily at a Eucharistic Concelebration with Members of the International Theological Commission," October 6, 2006.

———. Homily for Vespers at the Church of the Charterhouse of Serra San Bruno, October 9, 2011.

———. Message for the Forty-Sixth World Day of Communication: Silence and Word: Path of Evangelization, January 24, 2012.

———. Encyclical letter *Spe Salvi* (November 30, 2007).

———. Post-synodal apostolic exhortation *Verbum Domini* (September 30, 2010).

Bonaventure, St. *The Major Legend.* In *The Founder*, edited by Regis J. Armstrong, J. A. Wayne Hellmann, and William J. Short, 525–683. Vol. 2 of *Francis of Assisi: Early Documents.* New York: New City Press, 2008.

Carstens, Christopher. *A Devotional Journey into the Mass: How Mass Can Become a Time of Grace, Nourishment, and Devotion.* Manchester, NH: Sophia Institute Press, 2017.

Casey, Michael. *Sacred Reading: The Ancient Art of Lectio Divina.* Liguori, MO: Triumph Books, 1996.

Cavalletti, Sofia. *The Religious Potential of the Child: Experiencing Scripture and Liturgy with Young Children.* 3rd edition. Chicago: Liturgy Training Publications, 2020.

Clear, James. *Atomic Habits: Tiny Changes, Remarkable Results: An Easy and Proven Way to Build Good Habits and Break Bad Ones.* New York: Avery, 2018.

Cona, Louis A. "Stem Cell Therapy for Heart Failure." *Stem Cell Blog by DVC,* April 24, 2023. https://www.dvcstem.com/post/stem-cells-reverse-heart-disease.

Cook, Alison. "3 Hacks to Feel Better Fast." *The Best of You* (blog), December 5, 2019. https://www.dralisoncook.com/3-hacks-to-feel-better-fast/.

Cox, Trevor. "Quietest Places in the World." *American Scientist* 102, no. 5 (September–October 2014): 382–385.

Crete, Gerry Ken. *Litanies of the Heart: Relieving Post-Traumatic Stress and Calming Anxiety through Healing Our Parts.* Manchester, NH: Sophia Institute Press, 2024.

Cyprian, Epistle 62. Translated by Robert Ernest Wallis. In *Ante-Nicene Fathers,* edited by Alexander Roberts, James Donaldson, and A. Cleveland Coxe, vol. 5. Buffalo, NY: Christian Literature Publishing, 1885. Revised and edited for New Advent by Kevin Knight, 2009. http://newadvent.org/fathers/050662.htm.

de Lassus, Dysmas. *Abuses in the Religious Life and the Path to Healing.* Manchester, NH: Sophia Institute Press, 2023.

Francis, Pope. Address to the Monks of the Benedictine Confederation, April 19, 2018.

———. Apostolic letter *Desiderio Desideravi* (June 29, 2022).

———. General Audience. Catechesis on discernment 14: Spiritual Accompaniment. January 4, 2023.

———. Homily at the Chrism Mass for the Diocese of Rome, March 28, 2013.

———. Message for the Fiftieth World Day of Communication on Communication and Mercy: A Fruitful Encounter," January 24, 2016.

Garrigou-Lagrange, Rev. Réginald, O.P. *The Three Ages of the Interior Life: Prelude of Eternal Life.* Translated by Sr. M. Timothea Doyle, O.P. Vol. 1. Saint Louis: B. Herder, 1947.

Glaser, Judith E. *Conversational Intelligence: How Great Leaders Build Trust and Get Extraordinary Results.* New York: Bibliomation, 2014.

Gregory the Great, Pope St. *The Life and Miracles of Saint Benedict: Book Two of the Dialogorum Libri Quatuor.* Edited by the Benedictine Monks of Subiaco. Subiaco, Italy: Tipografia Editrice Santa Scholastica, 2023.

Guardini, Romano, Joseph Ratzinger, and Robert Sarah. *The Spirit of the Liturgy: Commemorative Edition.* San Francisco: Ignatius Press, 2018.

Guéranger, Prosper. *Explanation of the Prayers and Ceremonies of Holy Mass.* Translated by L. Shepherd. Worcestershire, UK: Stanbrook Abbey, 1885.

Hari, Johann. *Stolen Focus: Why You Can't Pay Attention—and How to Think Deeply Again.* New York: Crown, 2023.

Hicks, Boniface. "The Quiet That Speaks—The Silent Prayers of the Priest at Mass." *Adoremus* (blog), July 15, 2021. https://adoremus.org/2021/07/the-quiet-that-speaks-the-silent-prayers-of-the-priest-at-mass/.

Holmes, Michael William. *The Apostolic Fathers: Greek Texts and English Translations.* Updated ed. Grand Rapids, MI: Baker Books, 1999.

Houselander, Caryll. *The Reed of God.* Notre Dame, IN: Christian Classics, 2006.

John Paul II, Pope St. Address to the Bishops of the Episcopal Conference of the United States of America (Washington, Oregon, Idaho, Montana, and Alaska), October 9, 1998.

——. Encyclical letter *Ecclesia de Eucharistia* (April 17, 2003).

——. Homily at the Closing Mass of the Seventeenth World Youth Day in Toronto, Canada, July 28, 2002.

——. *Man and Woman He Created Them: A Theology of the Body.* Translated by Michael Waldstein. Boston: Pauline Books and Media, 2006.

——. Apostolic exhortation *Redemptoris Custos.* August 15, 1989.

Jungmann, Josef Andreas. *The Mass of the Roman Rite: Its Origins and Development (Missarum Sollemnia).* 2 vols. Westminster, MD: Christian Classics, 1986.

Leiva-Merikakis, Erasmo. *Fire of Mercy, Heart of the Word: Meditations on the Gospel according to St. Matthew.* Vol. 2. San Francisco: Ignatius Press, 2003. Kindle.

Marini, Monsignor Guido. *La Liturgie: Gloire de Dieu, Sanctification de l'homme.* Perpignan, France: Artège, 2013.

Meconi, David Vincent, and Carl Olson. *Called to be the Children of God.* San Francisco: Ignatius Press, 2016.

Mitch, Curtis, and Scott Hahn, eds. *Ignatius Catholic Study Bible: New Testament, Second Catholic Edition.* San Francisco: Ignatius Press, 2010.

Mullady, Fr. Brian Thomas. *St. Thomas Aquinas Rescues Modern Psychology.* Irondale, AL: EWTN Publishing, 2022.

Newman, John Henry. *Discourses Addressed to Mixed Congregations.* London: Longmans, Green, 1906.

Otto, Rudolf. *The Idea of the Holy: An Inquiry into the Non-Rational Factor in the Idea of the Divine and Its Relation to the Rational.* Translated by John W. Harvey. Self-publ., CreateSpace Independent Publishing Platform, 2017.

Potterie, Ignace de la, and Bertrand Buby. *Mary in the Mystery of the Covenant.* New York: Alba House, 1992.

Sarah, Cardinal Robert. "Silence in the Liturgy." Translated by Michael J. Miller. *Catholic World Report,* February 10, 2016. https://www.catholicworldreport.com/2016/02/10/silence-in -the-liturgy.

Sarah, Cardinal Robert, and Nicolas Diat. *The Power of Silence: Against the Dictatorship of Noise.* San Francisco: Ignatius Press, 2017.

Second Vatican Council. Dogmatic Constitution on Divine Revelation *Dei Verbum* (November 18, 1965).

Spitzer, Robert. "Rudolf Otto's 'Mysterium Tremendum et Fascinans' of the Numinous Experience." *Magis Center Blog,* May 10, 2023. https://www.magiscenter.com/blog/mysterium -tremendum-et-fascinans-numen.

Thérèse of Lisieux, St. *Story of a Soul: Study Edition.* Edited by Marc Foley. Translated by John Clarke. Washington, DC: ICS Publications, 2005.

Van der Kolk, Bessel A. *The Body Keeps the Score: Brain, Mind, and Body in the Healing of Trauma.* New York: Penguin Books, 2015.

Vanstone, W. H. *The Stature of Waiting.* New York: Morehouse Publishing, 2006.

Walsh, Milton T. *In Memory of Me: A Meditation on the Roman Canon.* San Francisco: Ignatius Press, 2011.

Williams, Forrest. "Review of *Silence: The Phenomenon and Its Ontological Significance* by Bernard P. Dauenhauer." *Philosophical Topics* 12, no. 3 (Winter 1981): 236–240.

About the Author

Fr. Boniface Hicks, O.S.B., is a Benedictine monk of Saint Vincent Archabbey in Latrobe, Pennsylvania. He has provided spiritual direction for many men and women, including married couples, seminarians, consecrated religious, and priests. He completed a Ph.D. in computer science from Penn State University and a licentiate in Sacred Theology from the Angelicum. He is an on-air contributor for We Are One Body Catholic Radio and has recorded thousands of radio programs on theology and the spiritual life. He has extensive experience as a retreat master for laity, consecrated religious, and priests. He serves Saint Vincent Seminary as the director for Spiritual Formation and the director of the Institute for Ministry Formation. He authored the books *Through the Heart of St. Joseph* and *The Fruit of Her Womb*, and he co-authored, along with Fr. Thomas Acklin, the books *Spiritual Direction* and *Personal Prayer*.

Sophia Institute

Sophia Institute is a nonprofit institution that seeks to nurture the spiritual, moral, and cultural life of souls and to spread the gospel of Christ in conformity with the authentic teachings of the Roman Catholic Church.

Sophia Institute Press fulfills this mission by offering translations, reprints, and new publications that afford readers a rich source of the enduring wisdom of mankind.

Sophia Institute also operates the popular online resource CatholicExchange.com. *Catholic Exchange* provides world news from a Catholic perspective as well as daily devotionals and articles that will help readers to grow in holiness and live a life consistent with the teachings of the Church.

In 2013, Sophia Institute launched Sophia Institute for Teachers to renew and rebuild Catholic culture through service to Catholic education. With the goal of nurturing the spiritual, moral, and cultural life of souls, and an abiding respect for the role and work of teachers, we strive to provide materials and programs that are at once enlightening to the mind and ennobling to the heart; faithful and complete, as well as useful and practical.

Sophia Institute gratefully recognizes the Solidarity Association for preserving and encouraging the growth of our apostolate over the course of many years. Without their generous and timely support, this book would not be in your hands.

www.SophiaInstitute.com
www.CatholicExchange.com
www.SophiaInstituteforTeachers.org